...ECHNIC ...MPTON 627781

Main site: ROBERT SCOTT LIBRARY. St. Peter's Sa..
Wolverhampton WV1 1RH

BUSINESS & MANAGEMENT
Wolverhampton Polytechnic,
Compton Park, Compton Roa..
Wolverhampton WV3 9DX Te..

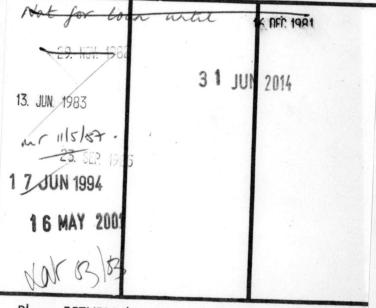

Not for loan until		16 DEC. 1981
29. NOV. 1982	31 JUN 2014	
13. JUN. 1983		
mr 11/5/87		
23. SEP. 1986		
17 JUN 1994		
16 MAY 2001		
Nov 03/03		

Please RETURN this item on or before the last date shown above   L·I

WITHDRAWN

A Short
History of
Taxation

B.E.V. Sabine M.A.
formerly an Inspector of Taxes
now with Deloitte, Haskins & Sells

This publication marks The Golden Jubilee of
The Institute of Taxation, which was founded on 5 December, 1930

London
Butterworths
1980

England London	Butterworth & Co (Publishers) Ltd 88 Kingsway WC2B 6AB
Australia Sydney	Butterworths Pty Ltd 586 Pacific Highway, Chatswood NSW 2067 Also at Melbourne, Brisbane, Adelaide and Perth
Canada Toronto	Butterworth & Co (Canada) Ltd 2265 Midland Avenue, Scarborough M1P 4S1
New Zealand Wellington	Butterworths of New Zealnd Ltd 75–85 Customhouse Quay
South Africa Durban	Butterworth & Co (South Africa) (Pty) Ltd 152–154 Gale Street
USA Boston	Butterworth (Publishers) Inc 10 Tower Office Park, Woburn, Mass 01801

© B.E.V. Sabine, MA

ISBN 0 406 53520 5

Typeset by Scribe Design Ltd, Gillingham, Kent
Printed and bound in Great Britain by
Biddles Ltd, Guildford & Kings Lynn

Introduction

A "Short History of Taxation" may seem a somewhat apologetic title. Indeed, why a history of taxation at all since it might be assumed from the indexes of the great public libraries that there was enough miscellaneous fiscal information for any mortal man, to use Sam Weller's phrase. In fact, however, although there is plenty of material, it is either highly technical or scattered at random by social, economic or political historians in their works as the context prescribes. This is not surprising since they have no mandate to chart the development of taxation except on the occasions when it becomes a major issue.

Taxation is part of the price of civilisation: for while it is possible to have government without taxation it is not possible to have taxation without government. It was, therefore, a comparatively late arrival on the scene of social development: for man the hunter, man the farmer and man the villager remained for the most part in happy ignorance of any form of taxation.

So taxation, when it began, usually as a tribute to the priest for interpreting the terror and mysteries of nature, would have a common origin: and the solutions applied for the raising of revenue would not greatly vary. The crisis of solvency is probably the most consistent administrative crisis in the course of history. Egyptian, Greek and even Roman financial contributions however, even though the Eagles were in Britain for four centuries, had no direct effect on British taxation which only developed its domestic principles, based on territorial units, two hundred years after the departure of the legions. This fiscal organisation was closely parallelled by that of the Normans so that the Conquest simply added to the indigenous systems the trappings of continental feudalism.

But both the old Saxon levies and the new Norman dues, even when bolstered by contributions from the Church and receipts from the royal demesne began to prove inadequate in the face of inflation and increasing administrative costs. The future perhaps lay with the voluntary contribution in the form of various aids as taxation began to pass from the provincial to the national stage: even more important an element of consent could now be discerned. Financial improvisation, financial experiment and even financial malpractice were the royal solutions to threatened insolvency: happily customs emerged as the mainstay of the revenue.

Under the Tudors the secularisation of government, including the Treasury, was completed, but even with earlier reforms and the spoils of the monasteries, beneath the glamour of the Elizabethan scene lay a patchwork and obsolescent financial system, which collapsed when the Stuarts forsook political acumen for financial prerogatives. So the Commonwealth created a fiscal as well as a political revolution for now the ordinary taxpayer was faced with parliament in its unfamiliar role as tax gatherer instead of acting as honest broker between king and citizen. In the end parliament began to dispose of a far greater income than the Stuarts could ever have dreamed of. But at least the problem of who was to levy taxation had been settled.

The history of taxation since that time has been more concerned with the nature of the levies to be imposed than the reason for imposing them. On the whole the eighteenth century leaned to luxury taxes and exempting the poor on compassionate grounds. This system adequately financed a peace time economy together with the rapidly growing credit system but it could not fund the Napoleonic wars, the Free Trade policy of Peel or the mounting cost of running a modern state. This was the function of income tax although at the beginning of this century it was still mainly a tax paid by deduction and a very late challenger to the yield of indirect taxation.

It is tempting for the fiscal historian to theorise about the ideal tax system, after considering how the system works in practice. But perhaps it would be more discreet simply to echo John Stevens who prefaced his "Historical Account of Taxes" (1733) by saying that his work had been "collected from the best historians, as well ancient as modern: showing when the Crown was supplied and impositions laid upon the people only by virtue of the King's prerogative, at what time the House of Lords alone has done the same, and when reduced to the Parliamentary measures now established. The whole intermixed with diverse remarkable occurrences and a considerable number of particulars which never before appeared in print".

B. E. V. SABINE
Mottram–in–Longdendale, Cheshire

Chapter I

Conquest and Domesday

In the thousand years or so of raids, invasions and migrations which punctuated British history until the eleventh century, the Norman Conquest was the last and the most important. Historians have long argued whether the coming of Duke William marked a real cleavage in the national story. Some narrow the gap and lay stress on the elements of continuity: others widen the gap so that Britain is almost regarded as beginning again with the Conqueror.

In fact the country was ripe for the taking after the death of Edward the Confessor. The question was whether a kingdom, already Anglo-Danish, would continue the Scandinavian connection through Harold Hadrada, whether the overmighty subject, Harold Godwinson, would succeed by force of arms, or whether William the Bastard would justify, as in the end he did, what appeared to be the best claim to the vacant throne. The problem of continuity, however, is more apparent than real as the position at the accession of Henry I in 1154 shows: for by then both conquerors and conquered had united to produce a social, economic and political development unmatched in Western Europe. Progress in the fiscal field was equally impressive, which was to be expected from the combination of two advanced systems.

Normandy was unusual, by comparison with its Continental neighbours, in possessing certain elements of direct taxation and by the eleventh century it had also become one of the most fully developed feudal states in Europe, with military service firmly settled as the condition for landed tenure. In addition to the reality of military service, revenue accrued from the ducal demesne, from tolls, market dues and customs levied on, and reflecting, flourishing trade and commerce, from the fines and forfeitures of justice and from other miscellaneous feudal sources. All these profits could be regarded as indirect taxation, and, as with the direct taxes, some would be administered by the duke's local officers, the vicomtes. They would often act as tax-farmers, paying their master an agreed fixed liability which they would then proceed to collect from the taxpayers in their districts, and possibly more.

There was, however, no central bureau which could be regarded as exclusively fiscal: the duke's chamber or camera was, in this period, an office of all functions, although some connection between it and the later Anglo-Norman Exchequer can be traced. Certainly there was no important financial officer, still less any court official, nominated as Treasurer. The closest approximation to this later development was the appointment of nobles skilled in financial matters to deal with that sphere of administration.

This brief summary of fiscal organisation in Normandy shows very close parallels with the position in Anglo-Saxon and Anglo-Danish Britain. As with Normandy its financial machinery was very advanced for the age. The royal revenues consisted of the geld, whose assessments were admittedly becoming somewhat stereotyped, the lump sums paid by the sheriffs for the profits from royal estates, the receipts from justice and the tolls and tributes from towns. There was a definite location for the Treasury at Winchester and detailed administration of such matters as the check of the sheriffs' accounts and the assay of the coinage. The main difference in the two systems was the greater reliance in Normandy on feudal dues and in Britain on direct taxation, and it was this difference which had to be reconciled in the period of sometimes painful adjustment which followed the Conquest.

From one point of view the transition from a direct and personal system of taxation to one primarily feudal was sharp and dramatic. William was a ruler of genius, clear-sighted, ruthless and powerful as none of his predecessors had been. His original intention had been to foster an Anglo-Norman state as his patience with the pre-Conquest nobility shows, but the necessity of providing his followers with their promised territorial rewards, and the rebellions of the native aristocracy which followed, triggered-off the social revolution which he pursued with such energy and thoroughness. He found a country whose apparent unity was deceptive and he succeeded to a kingship overlaid by tradition and privilege. He was able to create a unity and a kingship which were real and living: but in doing so, by the time of

Domesday Book, the old nobility had been replaced by the new Norman tenants-in-chief. In his introduction of feudalism he did not altogether discard the organisation he had taken over: he used it and, where it suited, him, interpreted it in ways more familiar to himself as Duke of Normandy. Certainly there was an immense concentration of wealth in the hands of the victors: William held one-fifth of the land, the Church one-quarter and eleven of his greatest vassals one-quarter.

Continental feudalism was one of the most significant consequences of the Conquest, and because of the imposition of a new ruling class, a stronger, more closely-knit feudal monarchy was developed in England than anywhere else in Europe. In addition, as one historian puts it, "the tenurial change proceeded from the top downwards as the new king first enfeoffed his companions and his vassals with their honours, and they subsequently and in turn enfeoffed their own men upon them". The wider implication of such a social revolution, arising essentially from this expensive military organisation through individual contracts based on land, the effect on administration, justice, religion, agrarian economy and finally, culture, form the whole fabric of mediaeval England, for the time being a mere extension of Franco-Latin Europe. But already there were signs of development, peculiarly English, in all these spheres, and nowhere was this more marked than in the sphere of finance.

Of course the accretions to the royal revenue from feudal incidents were conventional enough but they were new and important. Those most commonly met were the relief payable to the lord for an heir's reinvestment in the land: until this was received the lord retained full possession. Equally profitable could be wardship, the receipts from land during a minority: the king also derived ecclesiastical income during a vacancy at a see or abbey. A further source of revenue was the royal right to select a husband for an heiress: in some cases payment was made by the unhappy royal ward for permission not to marry the king's choice. Age was the usual complaint since the king might cynically expect a recurrence of the problem, and the profit arising, before long. Estates were escheated to the Crown if the vassal were guilty of a crime affecting his tenure: similarly, a fine was imposed if a tenant wished to alienate a part of his holding. Finally there was the aid, an extraordinary cash payment which could be exacted as well as personal service: this was eventually regularised for those paramount occasions which were when the king made his eldest son a knight, when his eldest daughter was married and lastly, should he be captive, for his ransom.

This summary may create an impression that the feudal system had more uniformity than was in fact the case and there is a temptation to sketch it in bolder strokes than is strictly justified. It has been said that the feudal system was invented by Sir Edward Coke, or, in other words, it is a convenient shorthand phrase for describing in a legalistic way the characteristics of a society passing through a certain stage in its history. Feudalism was not a definite dogma and the feudal system, as a precise system, never existed. Feudal relations did not exclude social and economic relations of a very different kind and were consistent with either a state of order, as with William I, or a state of chaos, as with Stephen.

The evolutionary nature of feudalism is well illustrated by the radical change in its very basis, the knight's fee. The knight was required to serve in the royal army for a fixed period at his own cost: but the knight's fee itself was remarkably diverse, five hides (i.e. 300 to 600 acres depending on locality) being an average and no more. From the beginning there had been difficulty in raising the feudal levy of between 5,000 and 7,000 knights: there were no dragon's teeth to be sown from which instant cavalry, of the standard required, could spring. A contemporary chronicle describes the contingent sent by the parsimonious Archbishop of Canterbury as consisting of unfit men, poorly trained and equipped: it was fortunate that the Welsh campaign of 1097 to which they were consigned was not particularly demanding. Secondly, the originally tidy parcels of knight service estates soon broke up and a charter of Henry I records the grant of a Warwickshire estate to be held by a third part of the service of one knight in such a way that "he shall acquit his whole service by the yearly payment of twenty shillings". Liability from the establishment of knight's service on small estates must have been paid to the Lord direct as an additional surcharge on the rent. Scutage, as this commutation was called, became more and more prevalent as campaigning abroad increased.

The profits of this exotic feudalism formed a new and rapidly growing source of income. An indigenous and more ancient source was the exaction of toll at the ports from merchants importing and exporting goods. It has been ingeniously suggested that this mechanism reflected the tolls, dues and commercial customs imposed at city gates when produce was being brought to market. However that may be, it is generally accepted that the king gained the right to collect customs since he afforded protection to trade. However, since trade in the days of the early Normans was inconsiderable and largely in the hands of foreigners the income was equally inconsiderable. The

4

principal import was wine and a toll was taken by the king's officer from every ship having a cargo of ten casks or more, of one cask from a cargo of ten up to twenty casks, and two casks from a cargo of twenty or more: this toll dates from at least 1055. As with scutage this payment in kind of the prise (literally 'take') as it was termed, was soon commuted to cash to avoid the problems of storage and disposal. In this connection should also be mentioned royal purveyance and pre-emption, the former being the right to impress carriages and horses, and the latter the right to purchase provisions at an appraised value at a time of national emergency.

Feudal incidents and the embryo customs can both be regarded as indirect taxation. Before dealing with direct taxation, however, it would be as well to look at the position of the royal demesne as a further source of royal revenue. Its forests provided hunting and venison: the savage forest laws provided barbarous penalties ranging from the loss of bowstring fingers to amputation of limbs and even blinding, and income by way of fines. Its farms provided provender for the royal table. Its boroughs were the most profitable, furnishing rent often in excess of their fair quota of the amount due from the shire owing to the ease of collection.

Recent research seems to show that the hoary constitutional maxim that the king should live of his own had a much later date than the eleventh century and a far different motivation than generally accepted. In the first place the phrase royal demesne does not seem to appear in Domesday Book at all: this does not mean of course that Domesday Book took no account of royal demsne but that the conception of royal demesne in 1085 was nothing like so precise as it later became. Secondly, the already quoted maxim about the virtue of royal self-sufficiency could hardly date back to the Norman period as the income from the royal estates, extensive though they were, judging from later and more reliable evidence, could hardly have exceeded some £10,000: hardly a quarter of an average year's expenditure. Thirdly, the Conqueror did not regard the royal inheritance he took over from the Confessor, nor the vast accretions to it, by forfeitures after Hastings and escheats subsequently, as primarily a revenue-producing asset. He had his feudal dues already mentioned, and he could draw on the Danegeld which will be dealt with later. These lands were far more valuable as rewards for services rendered or to be rendered by the Norman soldiers, the administrators and the ecclesiastics who, under William as their royal landlord, would be responsible for the control and government of the vanquished country. The concept of royal demesne was as fluid in those early days as the territories of which it was comprised.

The position regarding direct taxation seems less complex. William, as has been pointed out, was familiar with some forms of direct taxation so that the practical convenience of Danegeld would appeal to him, and although it was a more elaborate fiscal weapon than any in his native Normandy the Conqueror handled it freely. On the face of it, then, despite administrative experiments and modifications elsewhere, the main prop of direct taxation was retained.

Even so, the transition was not simply an automatic take-over. Danegeld, in its pristine meaning of a levy to appease the Danes or to subsidise campaigns against them, was exacted at its highest rate during the reign of Ethelred. When the Danish dynasty of Canute assumed the English throne there were, for the time being, no Danes to buy off and the tax was levied under the title of heregeld. Heregeld itself was abolished in 1051 but it is more than likely that Edward the Confessor reserved the Danegeld itself for use when required. This need not necessarily have been annually since the existence of some sort of geld and its elaborate assessment mechanism was firmly established in the eleventh century fiscal system in England. William may have continued the Danegeld or revived it as a definitely annual tax. This is not so important, however, as the probability that somewhere along the line, arguably after the temporary substitution of heregeld for Danegeld, the latter had begun to lose its potency of yield. The units of assessment were already proving out of date, the policy of exemptions had been originated and was spreading, and administration became inevitably less effective. Increased rates soon began to mark the decline of what had been one of the most traditional and effective props of direct taxation quite apart from the fact that it soon became clear that this old-fashioned land tax could not tap a new source of revenue, the growing commercial prosperity of the nation.

This analysis of the tax and royal revenue position at the time of the Conquest leads naturally on to a consideration of how the Domesday Book documents illuminate and develop the fiscal picture. The great inquest was, of course, never finished and its terse, telegraphic style often makes interpretation a matter of conjecture quite apart from its mistakes and omission due to hasty compilation, although it still remains, considering its period, the outstanding achievement of any mediaeval government.

In its time, it has been all things to all historians, but in this context, like the feudal system itself, it is its significance as an original source of financial information which must be emphasised. Even now it remains an inexhaustible store of information about the economic, political, social and administrative life in the mid-eleventh century.

Although the questions asked by the Domesday investigations have been preserved, it is not possible to say precisely how the replies, given in triplicate and arguably notified in advance, were digested down to the various Domesday documents. Nor is it easy to find out precisely how the inquest was used in later years: certainly the original returns from which the summaries were compiled must have been discarded eventually when their original purpose had been served.

This leaves the intriguing question of why the whole exercise was mounted, and to this there is no one answer. The twelfth century author of the "Discussion about the Treasury" (See Chapter II, pp. 26-28) gave as the reason that William "decided to bring the conquered people under the rule of written law. So setting before him the English Laws in their three-fold versions, namely Mercian Law, Dane Law and Wessex Law, he repudiated some of them, approved others and added those Norman laws which seemed to him most effective in preserving the peace". Aligned with this reason was the need to define the ownership of land before the Conquest and to trace the history of the current tenancy, thus preventing the increasingly numerous enquiries into disputed ownership. So much covers briefly the legal aspect.

Domesday Book has always been regarded as a financial document, however and it has been argued that although all the land-holders of England are recorded, only such facts, such rights and legal relationships as bear on the actual or potential payment of geld are emphasised. Questions about rents, tenures and local customs were dealt with sporadically and unsystematically. The record is basically a tax book, a geld book.

Two generations of scholars have now made it abundantly clear that this is too simple a view. In the first place, Danegeld was only one of the taxes which the Conqueror inherited and operated: its yield was too inconsiderable to warrant the immense expenditure of time and man-power the inquest entailed, if its recording and revision had been the sole mainspring. In the second place, as the "Discussion concerning the Treasury" puts it "The survey is made by counties, hundreds and hides. The King's name heads the list, followed by those nobles who hold of him in chief according to their order of dignity". In other words, the information provided in the original returns, verified and sworn to by meetings in the local administrative divisions, was completely recast to give a feudal survey of England, fief by fief, which was of no use at all in assessing or attempting to reassess, liability to geld. But to secure a due and punctual payment of Danegeld was worth a gigantic effort, and it was certainly true that one of the forces behind the Domesday Book compilation was the need to see that it was paid not more fairly, but that it was in fact paid fully.

It is tempting to generalise a little further and to speculate why the Domesday Inquest was held when it was. Here again the "Discussion" is invaluable. "When the famous William the Conqueror of England, the Bishop's of Winchester near kinsman, had brought under his sway the farthest limits of the island, and had tamed the minds of the rebels by awful examples . . ." or, in fact, when he had completed the subjugation of England, he decided it was high time he found out precisely what his conquest was worth. "Fond, yea too fond, of avarice", the only way this could be done was by causing a survey to be made "so narrowly that there was not a single hide or yardland nor – shameful to relate – was there an ox or a cow or a swine left out that was not set down in his writing". The Council held at Gloucester in 1085 probably discussed the financial problems which had arisen over quartering the royal troops on the barons when a Danish invasion had threatened; and this may well have triggered-off a decision that the time had come to reckon not only what the old Anglo-Saxon gelds were bringing in but also whether he was getting an adequate return from his new feudal dues.

Historians agree that a detailed history of Danegeld could hardly be written: this is equally true of early taxation in general, but Domesday Book provides an immense amount of detail from which a fairly clear picture can be drawn of the king's geld, as Domesday calls it, twenty years after the Conquest, although Domesday Book proper can be very deceptive in relation to geld liability. The conventional liability to geld on the normal manor would be computed on the lord's demesne which the villeins usually cultivated, on the lands of the lord's subtenants and, thirdly, on each villein's holding of their share of the manor's territory.

On this strict basis England could well have gelded for some 70,000 hides, but the whole system had become overlaid with exemptions quite apart from any inevitable changes in holdings which could radically alter hidation. Some land had never paid: royal manors had been regarded as exempt; the Church had much territory granted beneficial hidation where the liable hides were only a small fraction of a total holding; demesne land, too, was often written-off as exempt. In addition forest land was exempt and so also was land with the sinister entry of "waste", often through Norman depredations. Boroughs were liable unless specially exempted although, as previously mentioned, geld was no real reflection of their prosperity.

Domesday, however, gives a record of the amounts of geld paid into the Winchester treasury from Wiltshire, Somerset, Dorset, Devon and Cornwall. Details are given of the expenses paid to those who took the money to Winchester, on the amount expended on money-bags, and of the wages to the scribe who wrote up the accounts. The geld itself was accounted for by collectors, whose returns were checked by the central officials. For example, here is a record of a single hundred of 10s. hides. "Of these the barons have in demesne 14½ hides.... And for 85½ hides have been rendered to the king £25.3s. The collectors retained 10s." This clearly refers to a 6s. geld (85½ at 6s. makes the £25.13s. – i.e. the render of £25.3s. plus the 10s. retained.)

Domesday also provides convincing evidence that, after the possible lapse of regular geld collection it was restored by William. The evidence for this is now generally accepted, the corner-stone being the clinching statement in Domesday Book that in the borough of Stafford, "the king receives an annual geld from everyone", but annual or otherwise was by this time ceasing to be the central issue. It is evident that, owing to the increasing growth of exemption, Danegeld could never again assume the paramount importance it had once enjoyed when its title was literally true. Stepping-up rates was a sign of weakness not of strength and marked, if not the deliberate phasing out of the tax, its inevitable fading-out.

The danger of attempting to analyse Norman taxation, its connection with the Anglo-Saxon system, and how it appears from the evidence of Domesday is the danger of overrationalising and applying the label system to an aspect of government which was not yet truly systematic. As mentioned already, another label 'royal demesne' has been attached to the king's estates too early in their history, and this is equally true of the conceptions of ordinary and extraordinary levies together with the divisions of direct and indirect taxation. These are simply convenient ways of expressing differences which were to become clear but which contemporaries would not have made and might well not have understood. There was a good deal of improvisation in Anglo-Norman taxation and an element almost of make-believe where theory seems unduly divergent from practice. Indeed the distinction between revenue and taxation was blurred as, for example, in the case of fines. If income was caught in the fiscal net, the

9

Norman kings would not concern themselves over the question of nomenclature.

Of the five rulers of England between 1066 and 1154 William I was necessarily the most interested in finance since it was he who had to engineer the transition from the old Anglo-Saxon system of direct taxation, to the new Norman system based on the king's position as supreme landlord. It is very difficult to calculate what the Conqueror's annual income was in any year of his reign. His income from Crown lands has been estimated at some £10,000, but these would constantly be increased by estates falling in by death or forfeiture and decreased by grants for various reasons, so that the revenue from rents and rights was infinitely variable. This was equally true of the revenue from the new feudal dues which had been imposed upon England, and, a borderline form of taxation, the judicial receipts. William was also entitled to impound the revenues from various churches, bishoprics and royal abbeys, although here again this is not taxation in the strict sense.

The remaining source of income was the Danegeld which, as already noted, had become an annual tax increasingly lacking in yield through the spread of the exemption system. William I certainly levied Danegelds in the first two years of his reign when he would be in need of ready cash. The Anglo-Saxon Chronicle referred to them as "heavy taxes": in fact the rate of these levies of 1066-1067 and of the following winter is not known.

Apart from these two gelds, the Anglo-Saxon Chronicle mentions only one other, that of 1083–84, when a possible Danish invasion by Sweyn, the King of Denmark, was feared. William I imposed a "mycel great gyld" of six shillings per hide. "The king, after midwinter 1083, ordered a large and heavy contribution over all England – that is to say, for every hide of land two and seventy pence." The incidence of this was all the more severe, coming as it did after the "mycel hungor" of the great famine the year before.

There were, however, two other gelds during the reign of the Conqueror. The first of these was in the first decade but cannot be precisely dated: it must have been before 1075. The evidence for this is the so-called Northamptonshire geld-roll which is notable for being one of the earliest financial documents in British history and for the appalling light it throws upon the devastation of that county in 1065, for no less than one-third of the hidage is recorded as "in waste". As far as the geld itself is concerned, it is further testimony that its collection in a normal two-shilling year had become reasonably standardised and that its assessments were based on the old pre-

Conquest figures of liable hides in each hundred. There is no mention of any separate enquiry or of any travelling commissioners with their lists of queries as in the Domesday inquest: also it is written in the vernacular, an appropriate medium for the local collectors.

The second geld was taken in the year 1086 and has been confused with the other oppressive six-shilling geld exacted in 1084. Corroboration here comes from the Domesday which was, quite clearly, the writing-up of an extraordinary inquest, and the account of the Survey made by Bishop Robert of Hereford which mentions commissioners being sent out to conduct an enquiry and adds that "the land was vexed by many calamities arising from the collection of the royal money". The fiscal policy of William I was then a consolidation of the new system of revenue from feudal dues together with a reliance on an annual two-shilling Danegeld which however, in times of crisis, could be twice or even three times that rate.

Perhaps the most significant postscript to William I's financial policy is the comment of the Anglo-Saxon Chronicle that, immediately after the coronation, William II visited the Treasury at Winchester in order to inspect "the untold wealth there gathered in gold, in silver, in vessels, in costly robes and in jewels and in many other precious things which are difficult to enumerate". In spite of a dissolute, extravagant court and male favourites who could prove even more expensive than the female variety, he maintained and even increased his resources, although his methods were rather more dubious than had been his father's.

Some accretions came through confiscations after rebellions, but the distorted use of feudal dues emanated from a remarkable alliance between William II and Ranulf Flambard, "the chief agent of the king's will" and one whose extortions, like those of Morton, have passed into fiscal folklore. Fines were pressed to the uttermost farthing: on the death of Bishop Wulfstan of Worcester a writ illegally directed the tenants of the see to pay a "relief" in consequence, the quota due from each of the tenants named being laid down; and the revenues of vacant churches were farmed and successors wilfully delayed so that the income might continue to the credit of the royal treasury. There was even an ingenious form of scutage when William II called out the national defence force in 1094, exacted ten shillings from those who obeyed the summons, then sent them home. As far as Danegeld is concerned, there is no record of any levy apart from that of four shillings per hide for the mortgage raised by his brother on Normandy, but there is no reason to suppose it was not taken regularly as in the Conqueror's time and that the chroniclers as usual regarded it as a normal incidence unless the rate rose above the recognised two shillings.

There is more behind the Rufus–Flambard administration than the mere accumulation of wealth by the former and of chroniclers' execrations on the latter, however. The immense interest in financial affairs presupposes the idea, and even the existence, of an Exchequer, and in addition there is the curious story in Oderic Vitalis of how Ranulf "re-measured England". It is difficult to say precisely what the implication of this was, but a writ of 1093 which directs the justiciars to assess the Abbey of Thorney for gelds and other dues to the same extent as any honour in the whole of England, with the same amount of land, was assessed. This may well be evidence of intention to reassess the geld which William I had never managed but which his son might have achieved with the help of Domesday Book and the current returns which he had available by new and scientific principles instead of its previously arbitrary basis.

The reign of Rufus, therefore, was not an interregnum between two strong rulers but rather a time when administration advanced steadily, when some form of Exchequer existed and when consideration was being given to a new basis of assessment for geld. The work of Henry I was to an extent one of consolidation rather than innovation. He even followed his brother's example by seizing the keys of the royal Treasury as soon as the death of Rufus was announced.

His charter, however, on his accession, promised to put an end to the illegal extensions of the royal power, and Ranulf Flambard was for a time committed to the Tower, with a subsistance allowance of two shillings daily. In general Henry kept his word and there were few complaints about his conduct in his capacity as feudal overlord although he also was not over-scrupulous about the vacant sees he retained in hand. Henry again was prone to interfere directly with the relations between lord and tenant and to deal with the latter in person.

Danegeld continued to be imposed annually at its normal two-shilling rate, but payment was slow to come in and the tendency for further remissions diminished the yield. This should normally have averaged £5,000, but recorded amounts show £2,498 paid in, £1,715 remitted and £146 in arrear. Clearly some alternative was required.

Happily this was already to hand. The Conqueror was always anxious to push forward the process of subinfeudation while England still lay uneasily under the Norman yoke so as to provide himself with a Norman garrison: but then, as the political scene changed to danger to the king from abroad and to a feudal challenge at home, the sensible course would be no longer to encourage personal knight's service but a cash commutation for the hiring of mercenaries. This process has already been noted both for ecclesiastical tenants and for tenants holding a fractional knight's fee, quite apart from the incident in the time of Rufus. Scutage itself is first mentioned by name in a royal charter of 1100 exempting Lewes Priory, which is puzzling since religious houses provided by the Norman kings had been considered exempt in any case, but it is proof of the fact that scutage was known before the eleventh century and that there was no policy involved in its application: it was in origin a strictly ad hoc measure.

The second innovation of Henry I's reign was the development of the Treasury. The origins of this institution go back at least to Edward the Confessor, who must have operated a centralised system of finance which would be continued and enlarged after the Conquest since there were the new feudal sources of income to administer, as well as the revenues from Normandy itself. It is perhaps not fanciful to credit the influence of Flambard in the immediate development of the Treasury during the reign of Rufus: its essentials were surely in existence by then, that is to say a permanent board of royal officials with a function far beyond the mere collecting and safeguarding of treasure. They would ensure that all the royal revenues found their way to the Treasury and they would determine, judiciously where necessary, what was due to the king.

There was probably some division of functions in the Treasury before the death of Rufus, but there is no doubt about the special-isation which took place while Henry I was on the throne. The position is confused by a plethora of chamberlains, some of whom seem to have doubled various offices, but it is possible to distinguish the three separate bodies which were broadly responsible for financial administration, although the Chamber and the Privy Purse to an extent coincided.

There was, firstly, the Chamber itself under a Master Chamber-lain: he was often represented by two deputies who served in rotation. This was in theory at least the traditionally superior body. The Treasury had separated out from it, and was controlled by two Chamberlains of the Treasury: later one of these became a head Treasurer ranking equally with the Chamberlain of the Chamber: it is not clear however when this comparative independence was achieved. Finally there was the Privy Purse, which was also managed by a Chamberlain and whose controller ranked in the royal household after the Chamberlain and the Treasurer. The Treasury itself was fixed at Winchester with a branch at Rouen, and it is clear from the

13

pipe rolls of 1130 that certain Treasury officials had done a tour of duty in Normandy although the Treasury there was nominally independent, with its own line of Treasurers. Small wonder with this organisation that the Anglo-Saxon Chronicle wrote ruefully of "taxes that never ceased nor slackened".

These complaints could also have been levelled at the additional taxes imposed to make up for the declining yield of Danegeld. This was now being supplemented by a rate levied on a county basis, and by aids and gifts from the various boroughs to tap their growing prosperity. Feudal dues and fines were still proving lucrative ranging from large payments on entry to great estates, to the payment of £24 by the Jews of a certain community for help against one Richard Fitz Gislebert: he had promised the king 200 marks for help in his suit but Henry always rated performance above promise and judgment went against him.

The steady development of fiscal organisation was abruptly halted on the death of Henry I. The period of anarchy which followed, so vividly described by the Peterborough Chronicle was also a period when, under baronial rule, taxation degenerated into naked confiscation, and royal revenues were diverted from the Treasury. Danegeld may well have been levied in the more peaceful parts of the country, although it is not mentioned and Stephen himself was mainly subsidised, apart from the wealth he inherited, by the richer towns either by means of aids and gifts, or loans which he repaid by land-grants. From a national point of view the increase in waste land caused a corresponding decline of national yield. Somehow the Treasury managed to continue: naturally no real progress could be made in the years of confusion but the proof of its vitality is that even after a period of civil war, like Talleyrand, it survived.

The period of the Conquest, Domesday Book and the consolidation of feudalism is both confusing and controversial even in its fiscal aspect which, although it is only one of the areas of change ushered in by the Battle of Hastings, is one of the most significant and probably the best documented: for the first official records appear in the revenue department.

The Norman innovations were both dramatic and impressive, tending to obscure the intangible, older traditions which continued to develop below. These innovations were active: surviving institutions played a more passive role but were none the less important for all their lack of instant impact. To say William I introduced feudalism is to oversimplify, but from a taxation angle he did inject a massive new source of income into the royal revenues which quite overshadowed the old Anglo-Saxon Danegeld, with its elaborate assessments: so much so that he was forced to investigate its operation by means of the Domesday inquest, although this served other convenient legal purposes as well. The result was inconclusive, and the tentative efforts of his two sons to formulate a revised basis were equally so.

However, the tradition of direct taxation was not lost. Royalty and its advisers cast about for some new source of revenue as the yield of Danegeld flagged through exemptions. The increased wealth of the boroughs was one obvious target for the aids and gifts of the early twelfth century: the other was the commutation of knight's service for scutage, although, in this period, its levying was more for military convenience than for purely revenue purposes.

The administration of all these complex sources of income with their varying bases was matched by equally complex developments in financial institutions, the separation of the Treasury from the household and the beginning of the process of transforming the Exchequer from a court into a department of state. There is a degree of sophistication in twelfth century taxation which is often described lith a surprise almost amounting to patronage. There is no doubt about the intricacy of the tax structure not least in trying to define what was taxation and what was some form of feudal incident such as fines, or in attempting to clarify the interlocking subsections of the household, and the Treasury, and the duties of their officers. The saving grace of the whole system was the comparative smallness of the operational scale; and it should also be remembered that although elaborate records were kept and accounts carefully audited, there was no attempt to direct administration in the light of these accounts and records. The craft of preparing statistics had not yet developed into the art of using them.

Chapter II

Angevin Experiments and Consent

In some respects, the long struggle between Stephen and Matilda represented the high-water-mark of feudalism in England. In any feudal state both the political power and the surplus wealth produced by the workers, whether farmers, merchants, peasants or artisans were appropriated by the monarchy or the aristocracy, and the post-Conquest political history of England is basically an account of the attempts of each of these contestants to obtain the lion's share. In the Norman period, the three monarchs had, as noted in the previous chapter, enhanced the power of the Crown and successfully quelled any baronial rebellions, but the balance tilted the other way during the period of misrule and overmighty subjects and the feudal lords then regained a good deal of the prestige and the resources lost in the seventy years since 1066.

It was the special contribution of Henry II that he not only restored the prestige of the Crown to the position it had enjoyed under his grandfather but even extended its powers by his judicial and executive reforms. King of England, Duke of Normandy and ruler of all western France, he was the better able to subdue the English baronage who found to their cost in 1173 that they could not defy the lord of so many lands. Even the long absences of Richard I (although he was personally attractive with his aura of knight-errantry) and the unpopularity of John with his constant demands for increased taxa-tion which led to the Great Charter, could not undo the habits of administrative obedience which had been developed under their father, Henry II. After the death of Henry I, the inevitable outcome of bad government was feudal anarchy: after the death of Henry II, the outcome of bad government, even under three successive kings,

Richard, John and Henry III, was, finally, the beginning of constitutional reform.

The restless genius of Henry II was peculiarly adapted to undertake the urgent reforms arising from taxation and tyranny in all their many guises which had so characterised the past twenty years. The devastation caused had gravely diminished the yield of revenue from all sources: the accounts rendered by twenty-four sheriffs only contributed a mere £1,748 from royal lands in the first year of the reign.

In addition, one of the main fiscal standbys was steadily losing favour. The gross yield of Danegeld had remained unchanged since the Conquest, but taking into account waste lands, remissions, exemptions and sheer administrative incompetence instead of bringing in about £5,000, its final product had shrunk to some £3,000. In 1162 it was levied for the last time under its own name, grossing £4,812 with remissions of £1,574. The reason for abandoning it is still perplexing, and the most convincing explanation is probably the increasing difficulty of collection. Certainly there was no recognised substitute and although it was revived again by Richard I under the name of carucage in 1194, 1162 really marked the end of this archaic tax, introduced originally to protect the subjects of Ethelred from the fury of the Norseman as the Litany had it.

Although there was no designated replacement for Danegeld, its position as a bastion of the revenue was taken by scutage, the most frequently levied tax between 1154 and 1272. During that period it went far beyond its original purpose of providing the king with a monetary alternative to the military service exigible from his knights in person. Inevitably, with its more frequent employment, its rates varied, tending to increase, its organisation became more elaborate and its pressure more onerous.

In the forty-five years of Henry II's reign, he exacted eight scutages, six of which were in the first decade. Their rates varied from £1 for each knight's fee, the weight of the first scutage in 1155, to two marks in 1160, then down to one mark, say 66p., a year later. The lowest rate was half-a-mark in 1162 and in the last scutage of his reign he returned to a rate of £1 but this impost was not in fact levied.

The most spectacular scutage of the reign was the Great Scutage of Toulouse in 1158, which was entered on the records as a gift. It was not exacted from many of the barons, probably most did their military service in person, but it bore very heavily upon the clergy who were taxed in a most arbitrary fashion. They were rated basically at double normal knight's fee, then charged in some instances at many times that.

Henry II, however, could never have regarded scutage as anything more than a fiscal expedient. The six he raised up to 1164 clearly did not satisfy him and gave rise to the inquest of knights' fees in 1166. The tenants-in-chief were asked for details of their current service to the king, what it had been before the time of Henry I and what subsequently. The intention was to revise these military obligations if there had been an increase during either of the two nominated periods in the service due: if there had been a decrease the original obligation would stand. In fact the majority of royal vassals had enfeoffed more, sometimes many more, knights than they required to fulfil their dues, but any attempt to establish new assessable figures reconciling with the new number of knights met with steady resistance. When revisions did take place and scutage was levied on the new figure, the additional amount was simply not paid and the arrears carried forward on the rolls. The purpose of the enquiry had also been political in that Henry wished to be assured of the loyalty and due enfeoffment of all who held by military tenure since he was about to leave England. In this he was successful, but as a fund-raising exercise it was of very limited success: this may well explain why Henry II took only two more scutages during his reign. An average yield of less than £1,400 might have been a useful standby, but if it could not be increased without unpopularity and administrative distortion, a standby it would remain.

There were three scutages in the reign of Richard I. He was not in the least interested in the theory of English fiscal development but simply in the practical question of extracting the maximum from the English treasury. His scutages could be classed as moderate at £1 since the keep of a knight was steadily increasing and they did not cover the hire of mercenaries, especially for service abroad. Increasingly a sort of surcharge was being imposed on the basic rate, for the privilege of not serving with the army: the baron who paid such a fine was allowed to recoup the money in part by collecting scutage from his vassals. This feature, together with the arbitrary taxation of the clergy in 1158, marks the movement of scutage away from its strictly feudal basis to variations on the general theme of compounding.

It was under John, however, that the exploitation of scutage reached its height. In his comparatively short reign of seventeen years he exacted no less than eleven scutages. The rates show no particular pattern but by the latter part of his reign John was attaining a rate of scutage double that of his brother. Even so, with the increased cost of allowing exemptions it has been reckoned that John would have had to demand a £4 rate to cover fully the cost of substitution pay.

It would have been possible for John to have raised his rates still higher but for the enormous variation in the value of knights' fees. Clearly those who held the poorer fees could not pay a higher rate, and even the higher rate would not go far towards tapping the resources of those who held the richer fees. In these circumstances, therefore, John elaborated on his brother's procedure and in doing so fatally corrupted the essential nature of the levy. When he called his host together, some of his vassals were permitted to pay the formal rate of scutage but from others fines were exacted far in excess of this rate. For example, John's scutage of 1201 yielded £2,468 but he exacted £3,026 in fines, and as the reign proceeded the fines grew heavier. In all John raised a total of £49,539 in fines and scutage, £27,312 relating to the former and £22,227 to the latter.

These were very impressive figures but resentment of the levy increased with the increasingly arbitrary incidence of the fines. Scutage itself was no great burden except on poor knights' fees, although its recovery from subvassals could be administratively inconvenient. An additional cause of discontent was John's technique of letting no opportunity slip for exacting a surcharge. For the first four years of his reign, apart perhaps from 1199 when the campaign was inconsiderable, his continental wars justified the tax. However, the projected campaigns of 1204 and 1215, for which scutage was collected, never took place it is interesting to note that the former was said to have been "authorised" by the Great Council, although this authorisation probably referred to the increase in rate rather than the initial imposition of the levy itself. The last five scutages of the reign were fully justified by the military position, and it seems that too much has been made of the scutage of Poitou as an element in the baronial rebellion. Although the rate was high, there were no accompanying fines so that the barons could recover the whole of the tax from their subvassals. It was far more the failure of the expedition itself which seriously weakened John's position and destroyed the prestige which he had built up with his successes over the Irish, Welsh and Scots.

John had developed scutage, by means of his use of fines, as an important source of revenue, but he had accomplished this at a high political cost. It was not surprising, therefore, that this particular part of his exploitation of feudalism should have been provided against: no extraordinary "scutage or aid shall be imposed on our kingdom, unless by common council of our kingdom" said Clause 16 of Magna

Carta. The most significant point here is that not merely was the consent of the common council of the kingdom to be obtained, but the procedure for formally summoning its members was laid down and for making the vote of the majority binding on any absentees. The general conception of the Great Charter now seems to be that the myth was greater than the reality, but as far as fiscal matters were concerned, the barons made very sure that their proposals carried precise and practical sanctions.

Their effectiveness is illustrated by the story of scutage in the reign of Henry III, although the provision regarding it was not embodied in the Charter on its first reissue: on the second reissue in 1217, however, a clause was inserted to provide that "scutage should be taken for the future as it was accustomed to be taken in the time of King Henry our grandfather": in other words, the evil precedents of John's reign were to be ignored.

The result was that only ten considerable scutages were raised in the fifty-six years of the reign, but even at their maximum these were pale shadows of John's ferocious exactions, and although the fine for non-service could be high, there was none of the heavy surcharging of the previous reign. In addition full collection was not pressed home: for instance, the scutage of 1232 had to be reduced owing to the high rate of the preceding year. Even if collection had been more efficient, however the total for all ten levies would not have exceeded about £30,000 which was the normal annual income of the Crown: as it was, only half this sum found its way into the Exchequer. For in practice the service due from the baronies had greatly decreased, although the knights' fees liable for scutage numbered some 6,500. What had happened was that after a series of scutages when not all the knights were summoned, this partial service came to be regarded as the total service and, like Danegeld when an exemption had been conceded, it quickly became a tradition hallowed by custom. In the event Henry III took no more scutages after 1257.

Scutage was an acknowledged feudal due and it was only when John tried to turn it into a regular and arbitrary levy by surcharging that the barons felt they had the legal right of opposition. Tallage, originally the lord of the manor's right, as part of his seignurial jurisdiction, to tax his villeins, was not at first adopted by the Norman kings and to that extent the royal demesnes were especially privileged. From the time of Henry I however, the urban population, who were not included in the taxation of landed interests, were already beginning to give aids, which were a form of tallage but distinguished very sharply from the exactions the king was also starting to take under the same label, from his own villeins, much as any feudal lord since the time of the Conquest.

This urban, or royal prerogative, tallage arose, then, out of the contributions of the prosperous boroughs and represented a tax parallel to the taking of a scutage on lands. It became recognised practice, since administratively convenient, for the king to institute a tallage simultaneously with imposing a scutage. By the time of Henry II both the feudal and non-feudal classes of society were in this way making their individual tribute to the cost of government. The strictly feudal tallage was imposed about once every three years and at first was relatively unimportant both in incidence and yield. It seems to have been extended to the royal vills and manors sometime after the mid-twelfth century.

The reign of Henry I, however, starts with the taxation of boroughs by means of aids or gifts although the latter, like the benevolence of later date, had a minimal voluntary content. The administration of these payments varied but the general scheme was for a borough to offer a lump sum, or, possibly if the offer was not high enough, the assessment would be made by the itinerant justices. This sum when agreed would be divided among the inhabitants in any proportion they decided, collected and given to the sheriff. This was the pattern of the early levies of Henry II between 1155 and 1164. In 1168, however, the whole country was visited by a small commission of justices and clerks to make the assessments which raised £2,019. The word tallage itself first appears in the rolls in connection with the rebellion crushed by Henry II in 1174, and in 1177 the aid taken from Colchester is called a tallage: the old names of aid and gift, however, persisted until at least the end of the reign.

Tallage, like every other tax, was often in arrear, but on the whole collection proceeded smoothly. At first sight it is puzzling why the commercial class so readily accepted a burden which, quite apart from its connotation of villeinage, could prove decidedly heavy. The main reason was that payment of taxation provided both recognition and protection. The ordinary merchant had no place yet in the scheme of government but was willing to purchase a certain guarantee of his trading privileges. The early taxpayer was to find that in his fiscal virtues lay the seeds of his political identity.

Richard I, especially in his later years, continued his father's policy of tallages. John levied seven general tallages in the sixteen years of his reign. None of these extended to all the counties in England, the most modest covering a mere eleven shires, the most comprehensive thirty-two. Yield also varied from an inconsiderable

£1,500 or so in 1203 to an impressive £8,276 in 1210, the tax being levied on cities, towns, royal manors and lands in hand. These last were a fruitful source of royal income administered by his agents. The total yield of all seven tallages was £25,518. The general practice was for the assessments to be made by the itinerant justices, the sheriff bearing the responsibility for collection. Sometimes, as under Henry II, lump sums would be agreed by the boroughs: at other times the justices would assess the contributions per capita.

Tallage had not been exacted so arbitrarily by John that it appeared in the Great Charter itself, because he needed the support of the towns against the nobility, although an attempt to restrict it had appeared in the draft articles of the barons. It was however gradually being phased-out during the reign of Henry III, for while John, as has been mentioned, tallaged every other year, Henry III exacted it fifteen times only in his fifty-six years, or roughly every fourth year. Nor was it now the correlative of scutage, for he levied scutage and no tallage nine times, and tallage but no scutage eleven times. Scutage and tallage coincided only four times. The method of levy, by means of itinerant justices, was continued and the highest number of counties mulcted was twenty-nine in 1226, three less than John's maximum.

There was mounting opposition to the whole system of tallage however, especially when, instead of being able to compound, which was the usual practice, there was, as in 1243, personal application by the royal officers to individual citizens, much the same as those made subsequently for benevolences: in the words of Mathew Paris "according to the will and assessment of the extortioners the citizens were stripped of their money". This opposition became open protest in 1255. In that year the citizens of London questioned their liability to tallage. According to now established custom application had been made to them for the usual agreed sum as a fine or composition for the tax. The royal demand was for 3,000 marks, but the mayor and his fellow-citizens offered 2,000 marks protesting they would not, and could not give more. The king then ordered either the payment of the 3,000 marks or an assessment per capita based on chattels the value of which the citizens were to attest, but this procedure was also refused. The objection was apparently not to the quantum of the levy but to its legality for, on being presented with the precedent of previous tallages in the rolls of the Exchequer and Chancery, the 3,000 was admitted as the town's true liability.

Henry III took his last tallage in 1268. It had become recognised that both feudal tallage and urban tallage were owed to the king, but a tradition had also emerged that he should not be unrestricted in taking it. In fact there seems to have been an informal restraint observed, although the principle behind it can hardly have been anything more generous than a golden goose limit.

Scutage and tallage were two basically feudal dues despite their extension by the Angevins beyond their original bounds. There were, however, three occasions when tenants were bound to give aid, the knighting of the lord's eldest son, the marriage of his eldest daughter and the ransom of his person. In the period under review all these occasions arose and all illustrate, like the two major dues already dealt with, how the strict letter of law and custom was waived or even ignored.

Richard I's capture by Duke Leopold of Austria, a vassal of the Holy Roman Emperor, in 1192 was an event of crucial importance in the international situation and the demand of a swingeing 150,000 marks for ransom reflected this. The normal mechanics of an aid could never have raised this unprecedented sum; and in their endeavours Hubert Walter and Richard Fitz Neal, the Treasurer, who had opened a special exchequer at St. Paul's for its reception, ran almost the whole gamut of twelfth century fiscal devices. There was a scutage of £1 on the knight's fee; there was a massive general levy of one-quarter of revenue and chattels on the whole population with an abatement of one-tenth for parish clergy only; and the whole wool crop of the Cistercians and Gilbertines was requisitioned and church plate generally, although this was often redeemed. Even so the total was woefully short, partly due to arrears of collection and problems of accountancy. Further taxes had, therefore, to be imposed including a carucage of two shillings in 1194 and a tallage described as "ten shillings and upwards" the incidence of which is obscure. Finally the Emperor had to remit at least 17,000 marks and Duke Leopold received only a pittance of his ill-deserved share of 25,000 marks.

There were two examples of the first of the two other occasions, the aid 'pur fille marier'. In 1167 Henry II took such an aid for the marriage of his daughter Matilda to Henry the Lion, Duke of Saxony and Bavaria, at a rate of one mark for the knight's fee and in 1245 there was an aid for the marriage of Henry III's daughter Margaret to Alexander III of Scotland. The barons could not refuse to underwrite this but they could and did limit it to £1 for the knight's fee. Similarly, when in the same year, an aid of three marks for the knight's fee was requested for the knighting of the Lord Edward, the response in general was disappointing and collection problems proved as intractable as usual.

Last in the category of recognisable royal income came the profits from demesne lands which, to an extent, could be budgeted for. These, apart from tallage, do not rank as taxation, although they are clearly relevant in relation to the total amount needed by the king to subsidise the government of the country and as a measure of the extent to which the king could be expected to live of his own. If the Norman kings could have maintained intact the vast estates which fell to the Conqueror in 1066, no doubt the history of the Angevin period would have been very different, but accounts of a royal rake's progress which dissipated the royal demesne is exaggerated as far as the years between 1066 and 1154, although many grants of land were made as a reward for services given or to be given. From the accession of Henry II, however, the farms of the counties and royal boroughs were known and stated and the government began to pursue a policy not only of retention but even of expansion of their demesne rights, despite the writing-off of the revenues from the earlier grants. This was important for two reasons. The concept of the inalienability of royal rights was not in origin a limit imposed on the royal prerogatives, but a protection against the action of incompetent or dishonest royal agents: there was never any restraint of royal alienation for justifiable political reasons, as in the immediate post-Conquest years. Secondly, a royal pronouncement of 1266 spoke of "the places, rights, properties and other things pertaining to the royal crown". The royal demesne was therefore part of the king's charge, not the king as an individual but the king as holder of the kingly office. It was regarded as one of his natural functions to care for his manors and make the most of them by good management and resumptions where necessary. These, of course, were constitutional and legalistic considerations: from the fiscal angle the royal demesne did not produce, in terms of cash revenue, anything like the amounts provided by royal taxation proper.

The taxes so far dealt with arose from the feudal nexus and before long were to become merely archaic survivals of a statelier past. The future lay with the fiscal experiments of the later Angevins, John and Henry III, although they had useful precedents both from Henry II and the organisation of Richard I's ransom to guide them. These experiments centred round the aid, not the fixed feudal aids nor scutage itself as extended by the system of fines but the aid in the form of a voluntary contribution which had marked flexibility of both type and organisation.

The idea of taxing income and chattels was already making its appearance in the twelfth century in the shape of a tax on moveables to subsidise the first Crusade. Inspired by the example, Henry II in 1166 ordered a levy of twopence in the pound in the first year and one penny in the pound in each of the four succeeding years on all moveables for the relief of the Holy Land. There was no exception: all his English and continental subjects were liable. The contributions, which were self-assessed, were to be paid into chests provided in every parish. Fraud was to be punished by excommunication, but it is a fiscal axiom that the oath of the taxpayer never has formed the basis of fair taxation, except when combined with some power of verification. The same procedure was used in the levy of a tenth of rents and moveables made in 1188 for the recovery of Jerusalem, known as the Saladin tithe. This time there was a precaution against fraud. "And if anyone shall, in the opinion of those presiding at the collection, have given less than he ought, let there be chosen from the parish four or six freemen who, on oath, shall state the amount that he ought to have stated: and then he shall add what was wanting before." All persons who were not prepared to take the Cross were put under contribution. Exemptions were granted to the armed forces for horses, weapons and clothing, to the clergy for books and vestments. The total yield is not recorded but it is known that nearly £6,000 was garnered at the Salisbury collection centre: clearly this was a profitable venture, the lessons of which were not lost on the Exchequer officials and their masters.

Richard I's ransom has already been dealt with and in any case precise details of the yield and administration of the direct taxes are lacking for his reign. John's reign marks the transition from a feudal to a modern fiscal system and some, at least, of the credit for this development must accrue to John himself, always fascinated by fiscal matters and with the sort of pragmatic and inventive mind to carry them out, whatever his shortcomings as a politician.

Like his father before him, John made his first essay in direct taxation under the cover of religion with his one-fortieth tax on "revenues" (probably rents) for one year in defence of the Holy Land: there was the familiar self-assessment procedure without any real check. He followed this up in 1203 with a one-seventh tax on moveables or possibly moveables and revenue. There is little evidence of the incidence and yield, but the fact that it was tried so soon after the similar Crusade levy indicates that John was encouraged by the results of his income taxes so far: especially as in 1204 he took a fifteenth from the property of merchants which yielded close on £5,000.

The so-called thirteenth of 1207 was the most important single

25

levy of the reign and possibly the most influential of the period. It was the last of the series on property exacted by John and the basis on which the great taxes of the future were to be founded. The tax was first requested from the prelates and barons meeting in Council at London in January: the prelates demurred so the Council stood adjourned until the next month. The prelates still maintained their opposition but the lay barons were unable to hold out and on 17 February writs were issued providing for collection of the tax. Its rate was in fact twelve pence for every mark of annual revenue, roughly 20 per cent. The assessments were made by groups of special justices dispatched into each county. The bailiffs of the nobility testified to their property; commoners made an oath in person as to their own income and chattels. Prison and confiscation was the penalty for false information or fraudulently removing to another place, or concealing any liable possession. The records give the Treasury receipt as £57,421 with £2,615 still owed and the accounts of two sheriffs yet to come in. The total of over £60,000 was more than twice as much as John's total income in any one of the first four years of his reign.

Why then was it not persevered with? There is no one reason but a combination of circumstances. It required complicated techniques of collection and assessment. There was marked opposition because it was onerous and unusual. Finally, John's worsening politcal position, with relationships between both baronage and Papacy and himself deteriorating, meant that England was simply not stable enough for continued fiscal experiments.

From 1207 to the end of the reign, the taxation imposed by John's government was extremely moderate and the pattern continued into the minority period of Henry III, apart from the aid of two marks for each fee necessary to raise the 10,000 marks indemnity demanded by Louis of France. Although this was a large sum, nearly a quarter of the revenue of the Crown, it was raised without much difficulty, a clear indication of the country's prosperity, despite the civil war.

Of the aids in which John had specialised, Henry III, in all his long reign, levied only four from the laity. The yield of these taxes ranged from nearly £58,000 in 1225 to a mere £16,475 in 1232. Their administration closely followed the procedure established in the time of John. The sheriff summoned the knights of the country before royal commissioners: four knights were then elected to assess and collect, but they operated not in the district where they resided but in the others adjoining. The ordinary man swore to the value of his chattels before neighbours or, on appeal, before a jury: noblemen testified through their bailiffs.

There were significant differences between these aids as now developed and as exacted by John. They were earmarked for special purposes and certainly not regarded as supplementing the royal revenue. Fortunately they were not very strictly enforced and when, in the reign of Edward I, assessments were made to the gross value of the property, the proceeding was characterised as unusual and unheard of. Even so, the grant in aid of 1225, for example, tacitly assumed that the Council could, in the name of the people of the realm, agree on a tax which every liable householder had to pay. Taxation was ceasing to be feudal and becoming national. Finally, and most important, this new taxation imported the element of consent: it was a principle understood rather than written and Henry III was not the man to be able to persuade his barons that his needs and theirs were not opposed but identical.

Not all fiscal experiments were as forward-looking as the taxes on moveables, however. Carucage, a sort of revived Danegeld based on units of ploughland, was tried out in 1194 at a two-shilling rate. It was levied again in 1198 after a new survey of all the land in the kingdom which was to be assessed by local jurors under the supervision of royal commissioners, but despite this rejigging the tax was not a success and in fact brought in less than its original version, even at a five-shilling rate. Further carcucages were taken by John and by Henry III: it was last levied in 1224.

These attempts to impose a reformed land tax on a national basis failed. The tax was difficult to assess: for instance, part of the writ for the carucage of 1194 runs, "As you love yourself and yours, you shall so manage the affair that there shall be no occasion to complain of and inquire into the assessment and collection of the tax, to the great confusion of yourself...." In addition its incidence touched only the limited class of landowners and the Council which had authorised the tax in 1220 had not included all the barons, some of whom attempted to insist on individual consultation. Taxation could not develop within such a narrow framework.

The taxation of the Church is almost a special subject in itself. The king derived revenue from ecclesiastical sources in two ways. Already mentioned, the right to the income from vacant sees and benefices had proved very profitable to the Normans and the Angevins continued their tradition. By 1160 this source reappears as a part of royal revenue with a useful £420, the maximum in one year under Henry II being £4,168 in 1172; the average was some £2,250. Although not strictly taxation, the position of delaying appointment gave it a certain fiscal character, especially under John who showed a far larger profit than any other ruler. From then on the practice declined with the ecclesiastical Magna Carta of 1214, although there were some examples of quite flagrant prolongation of vacancies under Henry III. Winchester was void for six years, there were nine vacancies of two years or thereabouts and gaps of six months were common.

Secondly, the Church was subject to direct national taxation in broadly the same form as the laity but there could be considerable variations both in details and in timing. As an example, the clergy were heavily taxed for the great scutage of Toulouse, being rated quite arbitrarily. For the Saladin tithe in 1187 they were assessed as the laity and were allowed exemption on horses, books and vestments; and for Richard's ransom the parochial clergy paid only one-tenth instead of one-quarter. However, they were subject to gifts and aids, round-sum payments which, in theory at least, were voluntary; for instance John exacted a gift from religious houses in 1203 when he took a two-mark scutage on knights' fees.

Under Henry III a new pattern emerged. The consent of the Great Council to taxation did not apply to the clergy so there was less coincidence between lay and ecclesiastical levies. In the second place, papal taxation of the clergy and Henry's excellent relations with the Vatican led to systematic and profitable taxation of the Church, not without some resistance. The aid of five marks in 1230 from the clergy only was not, the king was warned, to form a precedent. The feudal aids of 1235 for the marriage of his sister and ten years later for the marriage of his daughter included ecclesiastical contributions. Tenths were also levied from all religious houses in 1253 and 1254 but probably none of the taxes for the whole period was as onerous as they might seem: as with the duties of 1259, the clergy usually had the privilege of self-assessment and self-collection, quite apart from the bargaining counter of composition. That was in fact one of the essential features of ecclesiastical taxation; the other was the factor of voluntarism and although aids and gifts like tallage could be arbitrary, they were tempered by the saving grace of consent.

Finally, in the religious context also, should be mentioned the unique Jewish contribution to the revenue. This can partly be classed under the courtesy title of tallage but in fact it was mainly naked confiscation. The Jews were completely at the royal mercy and acted as the royal usurers. Whenever public sources of revenue were deficient, the Jews were either tallaged, asked for a loan or fined. The machinery for their exploitation had developed in Richard I's reign after a series of anti-Semitic riots and a department of the Exchequer had grown from the administration of the estate of Aaron of Lincoln, the great Jewish usurer of the twelfth century. To John they were an invaluable source of revenue to be defended against everyone but himself, although the formal charter which he granted them was a rewrite of Henry I's. There is little precise information about the tallages they paid in John's reign, but from the references to imprisonment, torture, forced sales of goods and exile, they must have been of calculated heaviness. Henry III continued the policy of oppression, taking a tallage of 10,000 marks in 1252, although this sounds like one of the round figures so beloved of mediaeval writers, and another of 2,000 in 1241, which seems more reasonable. However, the Jews became steadily more and more unpopular; rightly or wrongly they were implicated in the silver speculation and coinage debasement in the two years 1278 and 1279 and finally, to complete the story, they were driven abroad, like the scapegoat of old, in 1290, a memorial to prejudice which was not erased until Cromwell's re-admission policy of 1656.

In contrast with domestic taxation, the history of customs dues was still fitful. In the period under review it was John again who proved the innovator. His first experiment was to establish customs duties on all goods imported or exported at a rate of one-fifteenth in 1202, and administered by three "chief custodians". They were provided with deputies in every port who appointed collectors to record the names of the merchants liable and the sums paid by them, with the power to arrest those who refused to pay or tried to evade the dues. Its incidence was probably mainly on Flemish merchants who exported goods to pay for English wool. By 1204, however, it had been extended to all foreign merchants, and £4,958 had accrued from it to the Treasury. In 1207 it was abandoned after John's truce with France in 1206, providing, amongst other measures, for free trade between the two nations.

John's second experiment was in 1210 when he divided the coasts of England into districts, each in the charge again of "custodians". This time customs dues were levied on woad, the old blue dye of the ancient Britons, now used for processing wool, and on grain. There is only a partial record of receipts from 1210 to 1211 and with so restricted a scope the yield was unlikely to be large.

The pot-pourri of archaic taxes, personal service, embryo land taxes and levies on moveables was served by an administration becoming increasingly complex as expenditure increased; and a unique description of the Exchequer in operation is provided by the

"Dialogus de Scaccario", the Discussion about the Treasury, composed between 1176 and 1177 and probably completed by 1179. It is the work of Richard of Ely, Henry II's Treasurer, and represents his office manual. The "Exchequer" (chess-board) is first described with its black and white squared cloth, on which the Accountant made his calculations using the principle of the abacus. He sat in the middle of the table "so that everyone can see him and so that his hand can move freely at its work". With him were the pesour, who tested the weight of coins, and the melter, who dealt with their assay.

The Treasurer however, was the officer who held responsibility for the bulk of the day-to-day business of the Exchequer relating to revenue: he received the accounts of the sheriffs and dictated the text of the Roll from these records of collection of royal revenue which thus became an income summary, including amounts outstanding. The Treasurer "must be careful to make no mistake in the amount, the account or the person, lest he who has not paid should be noted as paid or he who has paid should be resummoned".

The sheriff was summoned before the Exchequer bi-annually. In Easter there was a "view of the account"; no detailed record was kept, but the sheriff would be expected to find half the tax. At Michaelmas, however, the whole of the tax was demanded, credit being given for the payment on account by production of a tally, the notched and split stick used as a receipt. The sheriff would also have to account for arrears of tax and justify sums unpaid on current account. Only if he were sick, his first-born ill, or his wife in labour was he permitted to send a deputy. There had to be a special proviso whereby a sheriff could distrain on possessions transferred out of his area. Previously as the author indignantly records, a man could empty his barn and dispose of his cattle or hide them, before the summons for his debt could reach the county. Then, relieved of his wealth, he would stay at home, calmly awaiting the arrival of the sheriff. This is an interesting sidelight on avoidance as practised in the twelfth century.

The first and last impression of the book is the marked sophistication of the fiscal organisation. The hierarchical staffing, the precisely designed procedure, the careful accounting and meticulous auditing as well as the abacus-inspired arithmetic, all seem more appropriate to a much later period. A sharp reminder of the age recurs with a cold-blooded discussion of the forfeiture of goods after mutilation or the sinister recollection of the penalty for too little silver in the alloy which could be castration. It is a relief to turn to payment of debts by offering hawks. "If the debtor brings an acceptable hawk to the Exchequer and there is no one there to receive it and the payment is deferred, he needs only pay a mewed or a year-old hawk". Hawks owing to the king himself had to be handed over at Michaelmass "to be fit for the King's service in the coming winter".

However efficient the royal Exchequer might be, executive power rested with the sheriff, and it was John again who tried to reform the farm system so that sheriffs, in return for a salary, would render account of the various dues they had collected and pay all the proceeds into the Exchequer. This would have involved a complete reorganisation of local fiscal administration which John was not strong enough to complete: and Henry III had neither the inclination nor the financial ability to restart the experiment. No king had the temerity to persever with women as tax-farmers: the Viscountess of Rouen, who was responsible for the dues from Southampton, was a comparative failure so she remained unique. Apparently she was very much under the influence of a handsome steward.

The period from Henry II to Henry III is one of the most complex in English fiscal history. Briefly it saw the steady decline of feudal levies and the beginning of more flexible forms of taxation which could tap the growing wealth of the country. This transitional phase, in which John played a predominant part, was forced upon the state by inflation and rapid increases in the cost of government including the maintenance of the armed forces. The regular sources of revenue were failing to meet the needs of the king even when strained to distortion point: the reason why the duties of officials and financial institutions were so elaborate was that every silver penny counted; hence the search for new sources of revenue which, however, needed the vital element of consent, and a consent which committed the whole nation. The growth of royal power and of the royal household was constantly hampered by a lack of money which dictated such diverse policies as the thirteenth of 1207 on the one hand and recourse to moneylenders on the other. In the end an increasing part of the money raised had to be requested: in the principle behind the gracious, that is voluntary, aid, the constitutional struggles of a later age begin dimly to take shape.

Chapter III

The Waning of Feudal Taxation

The period from the accession of Edward I to the deposition of Richard II, covering the hundred and twenty-five years of the late thirteenth century and virtually the whole of the fourteenth century has not found much favour with many of the great historians. Perhaps the kings themselves disappointed, in not fulfilling the promise of their glad, confident mornings. Edward I, the Crusader and administrator, allowed his governance to degenerate into autocratic militarism and vain dreams of conquest. Edward II, strong and handsome in appearance, furnishes in fact one of the best mediaeval examples of the brutal and stupid royal gladiator: his supreme fault was that, being too idle to rule himself, he wilfully handed over power to favourites and officials on the make. Edward III was the pattern of chivalry, the successful warrior, who ruled like a patriarch among his nobles: by the end of his reign, however, he was deserted by victory, his courtiers and even his mistress, who stole the very rings from his fingers. Finally, Richard II, the hero of the confrontation with Wat Tyler in 1381, had a fatal incapacity to read political situations correctly and his alienation of the nobles led directly to Pontefract Castle. Until the rise of the middle-class, the king would always be faced with the tragic dilemma of having to rely for support on an aristocracy which was basically opposed to any extension of his royal authority.

Whatever deficiencies there might be in the personalities of the four monarchs, their right and duty was to govern, which became an increasingly daunting task. Disillusion and deposition were the occupational hazards of kingship. The complexity of administration was increasing fast. It was vital to preserve a nice balance between maintaining the royal demesne and the need to release it for income or reward for services rendered. It was essential not to let the bureaucracy, admittedly the most efficient in Europe, develop too strong a will of its own or a tradition of hereditary positions. Above all, to meet the sheer cost of government, the king had to secure consent for grants of taxation, however independent his powers might be in theory. Finance had become the compelling cause which was shaping the growth of parliament and which remained, throughout the period, the dominant feature of its business. This development was inevitable as the king sought for further sources of revenue outside the narrow confines of feudal aids.

The fiscal importance of Edward I's reign derives from his continuous and pressing need for cash to finance his campaigns in Wales, Scotland and France. This almost incessant warfare sorely tested the endurance and enthusiasm of his subjects and goes far to explain why his taxes were broader in scope and more onerous in incidence than those of any predecessor. The wealth of the clergy, the moveables of the laity, the goods of the merchants and the old feudal dues were all ruthlessly exploited.

Three features of the growth of ecclesiastical taxation prior to Edward I have already been discussed briefly, the profit from vacancies, the grants through Convocation and the royal share in papal levies. The first of these does not really rank as taxation but its use by Edward I was a significant indication of approaching insolvency, although by the time of Edward II vacancies were becoming shorter and thus less profitable. Finally, the practice arose in the course of the century of farming temporalities to the dean and chapter of a vacant cathedral see, and taking the right in the form of money. From then onwards both this practice and the receipts steadily declined.

The bare record of the grants from Convocation are easily come by. In 1276 the higher clergy were included in the laity's grant of one-fifteenth on moveables. Four years later, in view of the Welsh war and after discussion in diocesan assemblies, the northern dioceses granted a tenth for two years and the southern a fifteenth for three years, both grants thus being equivalent. These grants stood them in good stead for they were used in 1283 as a valid excuse for not making an immediate contribution, although eventually a grudging tenth for two years came from York and a thirtieth from Canterbury: a much more cheerful contribution was made in 1290, however, in return for the expulsion of the Jews.

From that date relations between the king and the Church began to deteriorate and in 1294 Edward I summoned the clergy to an assembly and demanded half their revenues or be outlawed. At this outrageous request it is said that the Dean of St. Paul's dropped dead. Within ten days collectors were appointed and, although it seems incredible, there is evidence to show the levy was practically paid in full. The Pope in 1296 had tried to insist on clerical taxation being conditional on papal consent: but in the face of opposition from both France and England it was agreed that this prohibition did not apply to a state of emergency. Finally, again under threat of outlawry, the northern clergy paid their fifth as a fine for redemption and most of their brethren compounded. The grant of a Canterbury tenth and a York fifth in the following year was a token of peace.

The yield of this Convocation tax is, however, difficult to estimate. Valuations up to 1291 were based on those made under the direction of the Bishop of Norwich of which there is no official record: from that time the valuation of Pope Nicholas IV was used as the basis. Then the collection of these grants was on a diocesan basis with officials appointed by the bishop, and although there was supervision by the Exchequer, the main procedure still retained its ecclesiastical character. Provided the king received what was due to him, administration was a secondary consideration. The average yield under this head during Edward I's reign was estimated at £7,500 annually but this figure may be exaggerated.

The contributions from papal taxation of the clergy to the royal revenue are, however, more readily ascertainable. They start in 1273 with a grant by Gregory V to Edward I for his Crusading expenses, but none of the coin seems to have reached England, possibly because Edward was abroad at the time. It is noteworthy that the Holy See reserved to itself one-quarter, a fraction which was to hold good in subsequent grants. The first contribution to the Exchequer came in 1278, with Nicholas III's allowance of over £16,500 out of the Crusade tenths: four years later the king's brother Edmund borrowed £4,000 from the Crusade collections deposited at the headquarters of the Knights Templar. Papal generosity reached its height in 1284 when Martin IV agreed to allow Edward six years' Crusade tenths which in 1286 was increased to twelve years by Honorius in spite of the fact that the king had seized nearly £25,000 of Crusade money stored in various abbeys, and that eventually the actual expeditions to Palestine were never undertaken. Finally, in 1302 Boniface VIII granted a moiety of three more years, with the usual reservation of one-quarter. The total was reckoned to have averaged rather more than £5,000 annually.

Clearly the collectors of the Holy See as well as those of the dioceses were hard at work on both papal subsidies and income taxes during the reign of Edward I. It became established that papal taxation without royal consent was contrary to custom, but Edward I, on the other hand, imposed taxation on spiritualities six times without papal consent. In addition he was not above an occasional lapse into sharp practice as, for instance, when he claimed the whole of the clerical tenth on the death of Boniface VIII in 1303 until his successor was appointed. Generally the pope recognised the royal need for clerical subsidies. The result was that the king could happily shelter behind the Holy See's mandatory fiscal powers while appropriating the lion's share of the proceeds.

However, a share in papal finance, however generous, was not a satisfactory way of maintaining a fiscal system: fortunately the memories of the taxation experts at the Exchequer were long and the tax on moveables which had originated with the Angevins was dusted off. It was a rare phenomenon in the reign of Henry III and in the early days of Edward I but it was used extensively during the latter part of his reign. It had been regarded as abnormal and its yield kept apart from the remainder of royal resources, with special receivers and collectors. By 1290, however, it came under the direct control of the Exchequer and began to play a vital part in shoring up the revenue.

As its name implied it was a tax on property which, unlike lands and houses, could be moved from place to place, and included large and small beasts, grain and other crops, carts and farm furnishings in rural districts, and personal and household property as well as cooking and eating utensils, jewels and cash in urban districts. There were nine such taxes in the thirty-five years of the reign, two before 1290 and seven between 1290 and 1307: the variation in the value of goods assessed ranged from a ninth in 1297 to a thirtieth in 1283 and 1306/7. Up to 1297 the valuation of liable goods was made by twelve of the "best men" from each hundred who were to go into every vill. Subsequently assessment was undertaken simply by sworn men of each vill: they were supervised by principal taxers and collectors, appointed by commission and able to call on the sheriff, if necessary, for assistance. They finally, under an elaborate ritual, rendered an account of their stewardship to the Exchequer.

As the pressure of these levies increased, however, the proceeds decreased from a remarkable £116,346 in 1290 to a mere £34,419 in 1297, although the former was a fifteenth and the latter a ninth. There might have been differences in mood, a contrast between the gratitude for the expulsion of the Jews and the war-weariness seven years later. There might have been more evasion: the burgesses who paid at higher rates had more wealth in cash and debts which was easily concealed and Edward himself had incurred some resentment over his scrutiny of all treasure deposited in monasteries and abbeys. There were also complaints about partial officials who assessed the value of their friends' possessions at below the exemption limit.

Arguably the most important contribution to finance in the reign of Edward I was the development of a customs system. This, as so many fiscal innovations, had originated in the time of John, although his attempt to impose a national levy was short-lived. Local levies persisted until 1266 when the lord Edward was permitted by Henry III to levy duties on the merchandise of all merchants: this imposition aroused such hostility that it was discontinued in 1274.

The customs levied in 1275, however, mark a complete departure from the type of general levy which had preceded them, being export duties on wool, wool-fells, and leather and hides payable at London and thirteen other ports to specially-appointed local officials under the supervision of controllers, a chain of command which John had used. The restriction in the number of dutiable subjects and the simplicity of the rates, half a mark on the sack of wool, or three hundred wool-fells and a mark on the last of leather, made the tax both profitable and easy to collect. The return between 1278—1287 averaged nearly £9,000 and for the last four years of the reign £13,000 or thereabouts.

The corollary to the "great custom" of 1275 was the "petty custom" of 1303, which granted commercial rights to foreign merchants in return for additional dues at half the rate of the existing customs on wool and leather, dues on wine, cloth and wax and an ad valorem duty of threepence in the pound on all other imports and exports. In these duties can be traced the origin of poundage and tunnage which were to assume such significance in the constitutional struggles of the seventeenth century. The average yield from these levies was between £9,000 and £10,000 in the last four years of the reign.

However, even the very considerable additions to the royal revenue which these new contributions made did not prevent the king from abusing them. He exploited his control of the wool trade by imposing a high additional duty, known as the maltote, amounting to three marks on each sack of wool or three hundred wool-fells and five marks on the last of leather, five or six times the "great custom" rates.

This tax lasted from 1294 to 1297 and was a prime cause of the constitutional crisis of the latter year. In 1294 also he ordered the seizure of all the wool stored at seaports which had to be reassessed at quarter of its value. The only consolation the merchants had was that at least the duty did exclude their stock from the category of moveables liable to royal taxation.

As more and more effective fiscal merchanisms emerged, so the old feudal dues began to disappear. Scutage, for instance, was now coming to the end of its useful life. Down to the reign of Henry II it had been the sole method of commutation for military service: by the time of Richard I, however, owing to the increase in a knight's rate of pay, a scutage of twenty or even forty shillings was insufficient compensation, hence the exaction of sums larger than scutage as fines, a process continued by John. Nevertheless scutage continued to be levied for another century.

Henry III last levied scutage in 1257. It was twenty years before his son levied it again, and then it is a debatable point whether in fact its revival was due to the Crown or parliamentary initiative. In all it was exacted six times during the reign of Edward I. In 1277 the alternative posed was simply service or fine since fees were no longer realistic. In 1282 service was taken almost wholly in the way of fines and three years later another levy left a fair confusion in its wake between service, scutage and fines. The highest fines were recorded in 1299 as much as £40 the fee, because the king on this occasion wanted service, but, not surprisingly, there were long delays in settlement. The last scutage of the reign was taken in 1305 but it is recorded that very little was paid. In effect the Crown was trying to convert scutage into a general tax, tempted by the fines procedure, a much simpler expedient than the diminished levy of scutage itself, but the attempt was not a success. Such was the hard lot of an outworn institution in a changing world.

Of the four reigns covered in the period, Edward I's was far the most significant for in those thirty-five years were laid the foundations of direct taxation in the shape of the fractions of moveables and of indirect taxation in the shape of Customs and Excise. It also saw the virtual replacement of feudal levies as a major feature of the fiscal scene, and the vital element of parliamentary consent slotting into their place. The extent of progress should not, however, be over-emphasised. Although he made considerable reforms, it is clear that Edward I was perpetually in debt, especially to his Italian bankers. Secondly, sharing in papal finances was not a satisfactory way of building up an efficient financial system. In addition there were alarming instances of corruption even in the highest ranks of the bureaucracy: there were the forgeries of Adam de Stratton, Baron of the Exchequer; there was the disgrace of William de Marchia, Bishop of Bath, and his removal from the office of Treasurer; and in 1297 came the downfall of Richard of Louth for corrupt practices. However, the most striking fact was that despite the harshness and the novelty of Edward I's taxes, there was no real resistance to them, for he had the ingenuity to use local officials for creating an atmosphere suitable to the levying of taxation and to invest his barons' traditional rights over taxation with the dignity of an obligation.

Edward II did not inherit an enviable fiscal legacy, quite apart from the sheer difficulty of succeeding such a king as his father. Debts totalling over £60,000 were outstanding at his death and the accounts of the Exchequer were in chaos. The customs receipts were mortgaged to the Frescobaldi merchant banking house, and the baronage, the armed forces, the court, the City merchants and the civil services were all pressing creditors of the Crown. In the honeymoon period, however, Parliament willingly granted him a twentieth of moveables from the counties and a fifteenth from the boroughs. There was also a grant from the clergy but the receipts from this would be coming in simultaneously with the last Crusade tenth of the previous reign. There was also a grant of additional customs. It seemed as if, from a fiscal point of view, the reign was going to settle down into the same pattern as Edward I's.

Certainly the progressive disuse of feudal levies continued. The last vestiges of scutage are to be found in the record of fines imposed for not serving in the army to march against the Scots in 1322. A tallage of a fifteenth of moveables and a tenth of rents was ordered by the royal Council in 1312 on the advice of Langton, the Treasurer, but constitutional objections were raised, loans were granted and the tallage merged into the grants of 1313.

This element of continuity was also exemplified by the contribution of the Church which amounted during the period to over £255,000 in clerical or Crusading tenths, and averaged £13,000 at a range of £6,953 to a record £23,016 in 1313. However, reliance on papal finance was a source of weakness rather than strength in the royal fiscal system, for the Church maintained the semi-fiction of independence, especially in matters of assessment and collection. Unfortunately the yield was too considerable a proportion of annual revenue for the king to be able to afford any quixotic gesture of independence, for it has been calculated that three-quarters of the total under this heading derived from subsidies raised under papal mandate.

As far as secular direct taxation is concerned, the practice of double rating i.e. the levy of two fractions in one year, had clearly established itself. Only in one year, 1309, was there a single rating of 1/25: the other six grants of tax on moveables were all double rating. The total duty raised was some £230,000, averaging £12,000 annually, with a range hovering round the £40,000 mark. This was a significantly marked decline from the early figures of Edward I's reign which had already begun to decrease before his death. It was a virtue of the tax that its yield was elastic and could and did fluctuate with the increase or decrease of goods assessable, which was a rough yardstick of the country's prosperity, but, as already suggested, the burgesses, who had more wealth in cash and debts, found the tax more easy to evade and probably did not make the contribution they might have done. It is noticeable that the borough yield, although at a higher fraction than that of the county, seems surprisingly meagre, usually at about one-seventh.

Customs pursued their steady but unspectacular course except for the flurry over the new custom of 1303 which, apart from that relating to wool, was suspended in 1309 on the merchants' plea that it had raised prices. Restored again, it was abrogated in 1311 to make a final entry in 1322. The average annual yield was £12,600 ranging from a maximum of £24,287 in 1323 to a minimum of £7,102 in 1315 when the famine was at its height and the government made vain attempts at price-fixing.

The significant feature here is that customs, a fiscal Johnny-cum-lately, was now providing an average contribution to the Exchequer on a par with the average of the lay and clerical subsidies. Its worth was surpassed only by the revenues from the royal estates where, paradoxically enough, in a reign which historians stigmatise as the worst example of the wanton squandering of royal estates, there is an excellent factual record of the first creation of a royal land revenue office which controlled the farmers and bailiffs and extracted the maximum profit for the king.

In view of the complex grouping and regrouping of aristocratic and dynastic factions in those political quadrilles which characterised the reign, it is not surprising that there were no fiscal innovations. In fact a contrary tendency was manifest in the sense that the Lords who had taken over from the king in 1311, for instance, declared that the issues of the customs and all other royal revenues were to be paid entire into the Exchequer from which the Exchequer officers would pay the king his household expenses "so that he may live of his own without recourse to prises other than those due and accustomed". New customs and maltotes levied since the reign of Edward I were to be abolished. This was to make it impossible for the king to augment his revenues by taxing the increasing wealth of his merchants. In addition, the magnates singled out as their vicims reformers such as Walter Stapledon, Bishop of Exeter, who revised the method of keeping the Exchequer records, and Robert Baldock who diverted some of the Wardrobe's fiscal functions to the Exchequer. However, by 1322 it was clear that even the conservatism of the magnates, as exemplified by the Ordinances of 1311, was not proof against the growing potential of a full parliament for deciding major issues, especially consent to taxation, rather than a mere baronial assembly. It was equally clear that even under a king as weak as Edward II, whose reign ended in a nice admixture of deposition and abdication, the civil service was fully capable of reaching a high standard of executive responsibility.

Early in the reign of Edward III, English ambitions were diverted from a sacked and harried Scotland to the rich domains of France, and the subsequent hundred years of expansionist militarism, profitable at first but in the end disastrous, had a profound effect on English political and fiscal development. The mixture of heterogeneous levies, on moveables, on merchandise, on spiritualities, together with demesne income, all of which combined could hardly be rated a taxation system and which barely covered peacetime activities, let alone the Welsh and Scottish campaigns, was now to be relied on to subsidise a century of progressively more expensive warfare. The growth in the power of the Commons which resulted was paralleled by a decline in royal authority and in the end the king lost control over a revenue (averaging some £14,000 in the first ten years of the reign) which had failed to balance his expenses for the singular and ironic reason that it never had been adequate.

The inaugural omens were, however, favourable. Although the young king could only dispose of an income approximating to £30,000, and continuous borrowing was inescapable, loans at the outset were running at the rate of £12,000 to £20,000 annually, the interest and security being easily covered by the yield of customs. Parliament met regularly and taxation was kept within reasonable limits. There were protests against royal attempts to increase the wool customs and to impose the now archaic tallage in 1332, but Edward could afford to give in gracefully when he was granted a tenth from the clergy, which would amount to some £18,000 on his sister's marriage, and a tenth and a fifteenth by Parliament both in 1333 and 1334. However, there was a new plan of assessment for the lay subsidy in the latter year, which was meant to be temporary and a precaution against the corruption which was said to have prevailed in the tax assessments and collections of 1332. The Exchequer officials were now instructed to proceed by means of collective agreements with the people of townships and boroughs liable to tax; each administrative unit was to agree a quota and accept responsibility for collection. The grant thus became standardised, as the land tax centuries later, and lost the elasticity which had been its prime virtue.

This was a grave error when the pressure of direct taxation began to increase as preparations for war got under way. Tenths and fifteenths from Parliament, and tenths from the clergy were freely granted, stepping-up the royal income, with customs and excise, to some £57,000, but Edward had already borrowed £100,000 to underwrite his rearmament programme and had promised to pay his allies no less than £124,000. It was thus imperative to find some source of immediate revenue; simply increasing the wool tax would not produce the sums he had in mind. There had already been an increase here in the shape of a subsidy of twenty-shilling and a loan of twenty-shillings on the sack the maximum yield of which would be £70,000.

The king and his advisers, therefore, devised a plan whereby he would split the profits of the wool trade with a syndicate of financiers, their security being assignments on the wool customs: the optimistic yield was estimated to be some £200,000 ready cash. However, neither side could agree on the precise operation of this monopoly quite apart from the fact that it was undermined by smuggling. Eventually Edward commandeered all the wool stored at the entrepot of Dordrecht, authorising the owners to recoup themselves from remissions of duty exigible on future exports, but embargoes on such exports periodically delayed full compensation and wool merchants were forced to sell their "Dordrecht Bonds" at a crippling discount. Parliament conducted a rescue operation in 1338 by granting the king pre-emption of half the wool in the kingdom on condition that the remaining half should be at the free disposal of its owners. This concession he promptly used as security against further loans from his Italian bankers. He could not turn to the lay subsidies granted by Parliament since they were already mortgaged in advance to these self-same bankers. However, the cash flowed in so slowly that Edward lost patience: first to go was the Treasurer Robert de Wodehouse before he had had time to organise the new emergency measures. Edward then expressed the invariable dissatisfaction of the soldier

41

with the home government by a series of regulations which reflected the extraordinary financial difficulties of the time: he even asked Council to explore the potential yield of scutage and other feudal dues, evidence of the financial straits to which he had been reduced.

Unilateral action, however, failed: Edward therefore appealed for a grant of taxation in 1339 which was given "in the way in which tithes were rendered to Holy Church, sheaves, wool and sheep, for two years". These would be collected and sold locally using the machinery of supervisors and receivers appointed for every shire and Edward made his usual large assignments in anticipation of the potential receipts. The significant feature was the combination of Lords and Commons to seek abolition of the maltote on wool and a general modification of royal exactions. However, the royal debts were now an astronomical £300,000: the 1338-1339 campaign has been described as the most expensive in the whole mediaeval period: and so, inevitably, the king in 1340 was appealing again for fighting funds. Again Lords and Commons agreed on a generous one-ninth from land and goods for both that year and 1341, and further, from those classes not liable to the one-ninth, a fifteenth of the real value of their goods. These grants, however, were tied in with statutory enactments which included the abolition of the maltote and of all unparliamentary aids and charges and the protection of the clergy against abuse of royal rights, especially during vacancies. The king had gained his principal aim in the form of hard cash but clearly the tax-paying public were relying on parliament to protect them against arbitrary exactions. For example, the king tried to raise a £20,000 loan from the City but he only just managed £5,000, the City's original offer being a beggarly £3,000.

He was now paying the penalty for embarking upon a campaign without the monetary sinews of war. The cumbrous machinery of tax collection was unable to produce money as quickly as Edward needed it, quite apart from the difficulties caused by "conspirators and false covins of certain wicked barrators". Events were now building up to the crisis of 1341. This was, to an extent, converted by Archbishop Stratford into a constitutional conflict between the king and his ministers but in origin certainly it was purely administrative and arose from Edward's financial difficulties and his determination to punish anyone who had blocked his supplies. There was an apparently complete victory for Parliament but this was more apparent than real in that any sanctions contrary to law and custom stood little chance of survival. In addition the king was perfectly willing to go through the motions of co-operation and consultation and to ensure that his officials followed his example. Parliament, as usual after its exercise in confrontation, came forward with a wool grant and a reorganisation of the one-ninth which yielded a sum well above the average tenth and fifteenth. However, the vital question of what should be done about the king's perpetual shortage of supplies, and the responsibility for the current deficit, was never squarely faced.

In fact the fiscal problem was never at any time squarely faced during the reign. Direct taxation reverted to the tenth and fifteenth after the generous ninth of 1340–1341 and was standardised after 1344 at a maximum yield of some £38,000. The tax was taken almost annually during the remainder of the reign although granted on three occasions for two years and on two occasions for three years. Extra-ordinary direct contributions were the aid for knighting the Black Prince and for marrying the king's daughter. The very end of the reign saw the clerical and lay poll tax, evidence, along with the experi-mental parish tax of 1371, that the old two-rate subsidy was un-productive and becoming obsolescent.

Happily the wool tax was increasingly proving its value as a bastion of the revenue. The difficulty here from the royal standpoint was that any levy over and above the customary raised the issue of consent. The period after the crisis of 1341 is the period when Parlia-ment gradually asserted its control over the wool tax, primarily because Edward, constantly in need of war finance, could no longer refuse to accept conditional supplies. The maltote of 1339 was still current having been prolonged by semi-constitutional means, but by 1343 parliament was making strong protests against its retention, while merchants were indicating their attitude by smuggling. Re-newed demands for restoration of the old duty in 1348 were followed by a specific request that the tax should not be imposed except by consent of a full Parliament, a point Edward conceded in 1351 in return for a two years' maltote. When that expired he attempted to get himself off the hook by summoning a novel form of representative assembly to sanction a three years' maltote. This it did reluctantly with the all-important proviso that its consent should be formally entered on the roll of the next Parliament. Finally, in 1362 consent to the wool tax by Parliament was unequivocably conceded by the king. In some measure it was a hollow victory since the king was able, in 1369, to take a maltote at the unprecedented rate of 43s. 4d. but he had sacrificed his independence to do so.

Although the decision that spiritualities were subject to lay taxation had been taken by Edward I, here too the question of consent was being posed. Ecclesiastics were reluctant to attend Parliament for this purpose since grants obtained here were subject to ratification by Convocation: separate bargaining was, therefore, found to be more convenient, but, as with Parliament, grants were often made subject to the remedying of grievances, and then not always paid in full. In general clerical opposition to royal demands lacked conviction, which was certainly useful to the government since clerical subsidies over the reign exceeded lay subsidies by some £90,000.

As a statistical exercise, the averaging out of the royal revenue during the reign is not of great significance since financial exigencies varied so much with the ebb and flow of the French war. Briefly, customs averaged £48,000, clerical and lay subsidies £20,000 and £18,000 respectively and hereditary revenues some £19,000. The striking figure here is that for customs, amounting now to nearly half the total income. More interesting, and certainly more original than these totals, was the attempt in 1362–1363 to draw up a national balance-sheet. Faulty in both arithmetic and accountancy principles, for instance in its treatment of loans, it indicated quite clearly, however, a deficit of some £55,000, an amount in excess of a year's normal revenue, a fact highlighted in an almost Micawberish example. Similar exercises could have been carried out either before or after 1362 but no trace of any other has survived. Certainly it may well have served one immediate purpose since the Parliament of that year was remarkably generous with its grants, but above all it illustrated the fiscal dilemma of Edward III, that it was wholly impossible for him to live of his own at almost any stage in his reign; and that finally, after his long honeymoon with his subjects, he could only gain additional supplies from Parliament or Convocation by sacrificing financial control. The nascent theories of consent and ministerial responsibility arose from the failure of a peacetime fiscal system to withstand the rigours of military expenditure.

To that extent Richard II was more fortunate in the latter half of his reign from 1388 for there was no large-scale warfare after that date. The state of the country's finances, however, was desperate: indeed on his accession the parliamentary rolls record a succession of grants in the first three years of his reign which exceeded any subsequent amounts. However, whereas the Commons were skilfully manipulated by Edward III and submitted, protesting to the last, now parliamentary conditions were becoming increasingly rigorous. There was a petition for the examination of accounts in 1377 and the following year the Commons showed a marked reluctance to make a grant: they complained that the large sum collected in 1377 could not have been expended and had to be reassured that the war treasurer had received the taxes which had indeed all been spent on the war. In 1380 the Chancellor had to explain the history of war finance, emphasising the immense cost of defence: in fact the Treasury was empty, the Crown jewels in pawn and the king in debt. Parliament accordingly granted a lay subsidy but specified how it was to be spent. After the Peasants' Revolt of 1381, and the failure of the poll tax, which will be dealt with later, taxation began to settle down again into its regular pattern of customs, lay and clerical subsidies and miscellaneous items, although there is a decided falling-off in the standard of bookkeeping.

Customs continued to be the sheet-anchor of the revenue, amounting to a third or even a half of the total. Rates varied little over the period. English merchants paid a surcharge on wool and leather: foreign merchants were surcharged rather more. There was a novel increase in 1377 of 13s. 4d. on wool, doubled in the case of foreign merchants, but this was remitted in 1378. There were also the levies on wine (2s. 0d. on the tun) and general merchandise (6d. in the £) which were doubled by the beginning of the reign and which remained at that rate apart from a short-lived reduction in 1390. There was, finally, a very minor item of butlerage on wine, a commutation originally of the rights of the king's butler. The average receipt was £47,734 over the reign.

Parliament, including the two poll taxes, made in all fifteen grants to the king, one double fifteenth and tenth, seven subsidies and a half, four whole subsidies and one half subsidy. The total yield was some £668,000 averaging £32,000. It is interesting to note that the yield of the tenth and fifteenth, fixed in 1344 at £38,170 was still yielding £37,000 in 1377 and £34,000 in 1397, although, of course, there had been a decline in the value of money due to the fact that royal borrowing reached unprecedented and almost ruinous heights. Convocation made fourteen grants, one double subsidy, one tenth, one clerical poll tax, three subsidies and eight half-subsidies, totalling £225,000 and averaging £10,700. Hereditary revenues are more difficult to estimate. Henry IV claimed that Richard ought to have been able, "without oppressing his people, to live honourably from the issues of the kingdom and from the patrimony belonging to the Crown, when the kingdom was not burdened with the expense of wars". This would be about £35,000 but loans complicate the issue. Richard had to borrow considerably in the first years of the accession, especially from London, but later, in a period of a decade, he resorted to loans only three times. This might well be because he had no compunction in his despotic days about exacting money by forced loans, crooked pardons, blank charters and the ironic device of 'le plesaunce'.

The most interesting fiscal experiment of the reign was the poll tax. This was first imposed in 1377, "a tax hitherto unheard of", as Walsingham put it, at the rate of fourpence "to be taken from the goods of each person in the kingdom, man and woman, over the age of fourteen, except only real beggars". To supplement this the grant from the clergy was one shilling from every beneficed person and fourpence from every other religious person except mendicant friars. The yield was £22,607 and 1,376,442 lay persons paid the tax. The next poll tax, in 1379 the first of Richard II's reign, was elaborately graduated. The schedule of charge classified tax-payers as follows:–

Rate	Classes
£ s. d.	
6 13 4	Duke of Lancaster. Duke of Brittany.
5 0 0	All Justices.
4 0 0	Earls and Countesses: the Mayor of London.
2 0 0	Barons and Baronesses and knights "who could spend as much". Chief Prior of the Hospitallers: Sergeants of law: London Aldermen and Mayors.
1 0 0	Knights and "squires who should be knights", their widows and dames: apprentices to the profession of the law. Great Merchants.
6 8	Esquires of less estate: substantial merchants, attorneys, franklins and other landed gentry.
3 4	Esquires without property, smaller merchants, wealthy farmers and cattle dealers: pardoners and summoners.
4	Every married man, for himself and his wife, and every man and woman sole over the age of sixteen except real beggars.

As far as clergy were concerned, the Archbishop of Canterbury was in the top rate; bishops and mitred abbots paid £4; those holding benefices paid according to their value and the ordinary monk's or nun's rate varied from 3s. 4d. to the lowest rate of 4d. The expected yield was £50,000 but in the event not half that sum was realised.

So far then the poll tax had proved a very moderate success. In 1380 the king requested a grant of £160,000. Outraged by this demand, after long deliberation, the Commons offered two-thirds of £100,000 if the clergy would provide the balance of one-third and the method suggested for raising this sum was a tax of one shilling from every lay person in the kingdom, male and female over the age of fifteen, except the inevitable real beggars. Everyone was charged at his place of residence or employment and persons of substance were, according to their property, to assist the poorer persons.

The reasons for the introduction of poll tax were two-fold. In the first place the Commons were increasingly reluctant to burden themselves, as the propertied and moneyed class, with taxes which touched only them, especially when the spoils of victory were uncertain and military honour as unrewarding as Falstaff found it. Secondly, since the economic dislocation caused by the Black Death, there was a growing feeling among the upper ranks of society that the common people were becoming too independent and too prosperous, and that a broadening of the fiscal base would be both salutary and profitable.

Against these considerations there were other factors which the government would have done well to ponder. Most important was the social unrest which the authorities were well aware of. Sir Richard Waldegrave, the Speaker of the 1391 Parliament, blamed the extravagance of the court and household, the burden of taxation and the weakness of the executive. Then there was the sheer inequity of the tax, especially the dropping of graduation. The course of collection only exacerbated the situation. Two-thirds of the tax should have been paid by early January but so disappointing was the yield due to apparent falls in population from twenty to as much as fifty per cent. that the collectors were written-off as either negligent or corrupt; and fresh commissioners were appointed to step-up the pressure which gave rise to a rumour that a second unauthorised levy was to be exacted. Finally, England had before it the unpopularity of the fouage or hearth tax in France.

Why then did the Government continue on their collision course which eventually triggered off the Peasants' Revolt? Clearly they overrated their ability to mount the type of enquiry which the Conqueror had made which can only be done by a primitive or highly disciplined community. The result was a reluctant or hostile populace resisting a bewildering and chaotic fiscal exercise in which one set of officials simply impeded the other. Basically however, they were the victims of their own simple, not to say innocent arithmetic. In 1377 poll tax had produced some £22,000 at a fourpenny rate: the authorities thought that a shilling rate would automatically produce the

required £66,000 without making any allowance for the unfair incidence of the tax, the inefficiency and corruption of the bureaucracy
and the temptation to evade. In the end its yield was about £44,000 at
the price of a near-revolution the demands of whose leaders went,
before the rising was quelled, far beyond the original grievance of Wat
Tyler against a levy which was not to be revived until 1513.

The years of the three Edwards and Richard II, years of battle,
gloom and sudden death, saw the emergence of new forms of taxation
partly because, in the violent times of endemic warfare, the king could
not live of his own and partly because of the built-in obsolescence of
the archaic feudal levies. These new taxes met with varying success:
the poll tax was a disastrous failure: the fractional taxes became
rarified into a quota. Customs, however, went from strength to
strength as the mainstay of the revenue, but the fiscal ledger, by 1400,
had by no means been ruled off and balanced. The struggle for
parliamentary consent to the levying of taxation had been partly won:
now the claim was being raised not only for control of collection but of
spending also.

Chapter IV

Wars and Taxes

It is now no longer historically fashionable to draw a sharp contrast between the despotism of Richard II and the constitutionalism of Henry IV. Admittedly in his later years Richard II showed himself capricious and high-handed to a degree, but he had neither the ability nor the application to become an absolute monarch. Similarly, although Henry IV grasped the throne with the tacit approval of parliament, no parliamentary conditions were in fact imposed upon him. There was no clear-cut distinction between the monarchial policy of the fifteenth and that of the fourteenth century. Henry IV ruled by the same machinery and through the same persons as Richard II.

There was, however, a marked distinction in financial policy. Again, in the latter period of his régime, Richard II, pursuing a more peaceful foreign course, could more than balance his budget with little recourse to loans, but Henry IV, although he brought all his income of some £14,000 annually from his Duchy of Lancaster as a dowry to the throne, was from the first a prisoner of the financial situation which the manner of his accession forced upon him: Henry IV's previous ducal affluence was no preparation for his new special responsibilities and increased financial obligations.

The fiscal auguries at the beginning of the reign were distinctly unfavourable. The Dartmouth tax-collector only managed to evade his enraged victims by boat: some cloth-dealers flatly refused to pay the levy on their wares and although in the first three months of Henry's reign revenue and expenditure nearly balanced, less than a fifth of the income represented taxation, the balance being made up of non-recurrent items. Nine parliaments in fourteen years were to represent his perennial need for money, the immediate demands being for subsidising Calais and the Welsh campaigns; but the story is not one of increasing parliamentary control over supplies, still less of a calculated campaign for restricting royal power. The graph of parliamentary opposition rises steeply to 1406, then tapers off to the last Parliament of 1411 when grants were made almost as a matter of routine.

In fact Henry's first appeal for money was to the Great Council since an appeal to Parliament would have involved taxing the Commons, a contingency he preferred to avoid so early in his reign. The results were disappointing: the Lords simply provided three months' service against the Scots: the clergy offered their usual tenth, but it was slow to come in, especially from the bishops, and realised only £4,000. Even customs, the standby of the revenue, were declining due to a fall in wool exports, and the Council summoned the collectors to report urgently on the problem.

The calling of Parliament could not long be delayed: the bone of contention would clearly be, as it was to remain, finance, but both sides were anxious at first not to press their arguments too far. Minor concessions were made by the king in his first two Parliaments in return for a not very generous tenth and fifteenth, tunnage and poundage up to Easter 1403, and a clerical tenth. The Council did some rapid budgeting and came up with a cash requirement of some £120,000 of which over half was for defence and loan repayment quite apart from the expenses of the royal household which had not been taken into account. Fresh loan-raising exercises brought £16,000, the highest total for any half-year during the reign, but this by no means filled the gap.

The Commons in the third Parliament of the reign, in 1405, put themselves in a slightly false strategic position by "communing" with the Lords before the first session. Henry was quick to remind them that such a procedure was a privilege and not a right. Perhaps on this account the grants of customs, a subsidy on wool and woolfells, tunnage and poundage to be continued from the last grant to September 1405 together with the usual tenth and fifteenth, and a clerical tenth was passed without the expected prolonged discussion and nagging criticism. However, there was a move to resume into the royal hands all landed resources held in absolute possession since 1366: parliamentary opposition was coming into the open.

1404 was the year of two Parliaments. Both the Chancellor and

Treasurer were at pains to explain the financial difficulties to Parliament, especially in relation to defence. Parliament retorted by claiming that the revenue from customs, Crown lands and the Duchy of Lancaster should be sufficient, especially if there were economies in household expenses: the king could not expect direct taxes in addition. Henry had to underline the arguments of his officials and stress that this additional revenue was needed for defence. Eventually, to meet this plea, they reluctantly agreed a unique tax of 20s. 0d. from each knight's fee and 1s. 0d. from each £'s worth of land, goods and other sources of income. So strongly did Parliament feel about this levy that it prescribed no records of the tax should be kept and no mention of it made on the Parliament Roll. It was also to be paid to, and administered by, four specially-appointed Treasurers of War.

By September the deteriorating political situation made Henry's need of money imperative and a Parliament was called at Coventry: possibly he hoped for a shorter session there as most members preferred to sit at Westminster. In the event there was a month of debate but the resultant grants were reasonably generous. In addition there was a second fiscal experiment, a sort of land tax of 20s. 0d. on each £20 of land from owners with revenue from considerable estates.

This levy, too, as with its predecessor six months before, was not to be taken as a precedent. The king could feel well pleased with the outcome of the Coventry Parliament's deliberations for he also succeeded in substituting the four War Treasurers by two more congenial. He also fended off Parliament's pressure for resumptions by the appointment of a committee of enquiry, a certain recipe for delay even in those days, being rightly convinced that the obvious political disadvantages of the suggested policy would outweigh the dubious profit to the revenue.

Whatever his political strategy, the king's financial difficulties remained pressing and when his seventh Parliament met in 1406 it was in an extremely captious mood. Its initial demand that the Treasurers should submit a reckoning drew from Henry the spirited reply that "kings were not wont to render account". Eventually he conceded the point in return for a shilling increase in the rate of tunnage and poundage. Parliament then adjourned on the 19 June "considering", as they put it, "their great labours, the needs of the harvest and the great heat, as well as their enemies by land and sea". Subsequently there was an attempt to make their grants conditional on certain lords guaranteeing refunds if tax should be misappropriated, but Henry successfully resisted this innovation: to an extent the Church came to his rescue with a tenth and the promise of speedy appointment of collectors to gather the contribution in. The Parliament of 1406 was indeed critical, obstructive and at times turbulent, but it had no formulated policy except the perennial attack on taxation.

As suggested, from 1406, roughly the mid-point of the reign, a different fiscal pattern began to emerge, although financial embarrassments were to prove no less frequent. In 1407 there was what almost amounted to a conference on taxation between the Chancellor, the Lords and the Commons, although the last-named were "greatly disturbed" because the king had consulted the Lords before the meeting. The usual grants were made but the Council was to have the major say in expending the resultant revenue apart from a mere £6,000 at the king's disposal.

The king's fiscal initiative was also seriously weakened by his illness so that from 1407 onwards many major decisions were taken either by Council or the increasingly dominant figures of Arundel and Prince Henry. Parliament was still demanding that the grants it made should be devoted to defence and flatly turned down the royal counter-claim of a regular tenth and fifteenth for the rest of his life. Instead they conceded one-and-a-half tenths and fifteenths, for three years as well as the usual wool subsidy and tunnage and poundage. Theoretically the summons of Parliament could have been dispensed with for those three years but in the event the yield of the grants was totally inadequate: it is not even clear whether all of the tax was ever collected. As always, there was no remedy except ever-increasing taxes, failing which the Exchequer had to carry on the king's government by anticipating coming revenues by assignment and pressing for immediate cash loans to cover day to day expenditure.

It is possible that the last Parliament of the reign in 1411 saw dimly that the desperate state of the finances was not wholly the fault of the king. The terms of the grants of taxation are not known but, judging from the preambles, the intentions were the most generous of the reign. Apart from the customary import and export dues, there was a reversion to the novel tax of 1404 but this time there was no veto on recording it.

The reign of Henry IV saw the beginning of all the fiscal problems which were to bedevil relations between king and Parliament until the final resolution of the Civil War. The element of conflict between Henry and his Parliaments should not be overdramatised. A general state of tension was intelligible in the context of the revolution of 1399: Parliament had not then connived in the deposition of Richard II in order to pay heavier taxes. What they had given they could at least try to control if not take away, but Parliament planned no financial reform nor advance budgeting: a favourite programme was the resumption of Crown lands. It was contended that undeserved gifts of land should be taken back by the king and that revenue from taxation should merely make up the difference in so far as the income from the resumed lands was insufficient to meet the king's needs. Frustrated here, on occasions, they turned to advocating complete expropriation of Church property: Lollardry however was never powerful enough in Parliament to make this a viable proposition.

The basic weakness of Henry's financial position was that while Richard II's income had been some £140,000 annually, including loans, Henry's average was around £90,000 with average expenditure running at the rate of his predecessor's revenue. He was forced to borrow, and chronic debt was a besetting evil of the Lancastrian régime, especially as Henry defaulted more than Richard and spread his loans less widely. Credit transactions had now become prevalent in all classes, a fifteenth century equivalent of a flutter on the Stock Exchange. In addition there was a certain measure of devaluation as well as a falling off in customs due to the declining wool trade. On the three occasions new forms of taxation had been tried, because the yield from the tenth and fifteenth had become static, the results were disappointing. The royal revenues were indeed "burdened outrageously", as the Treasurer wrote to the king as early as 1401: and although specific evidence is hard to come by, attempts from both king and Parliament to organise a proper audit system, to speed the ingathering of revenue and to check both the inefficiency and downright dishonesty of the collectors, testify to the haphazard nature of fiscal administration: and future revenues were mortgaged as a precaution against current insolvency.

The pattern of discussion and co-operation about taxation between king, Council and Lords in Parliament, accompanied by a running fire of suggestions and criticisms from the Commons, had established itself as early as Edward III. Sometimes this relationship was strained and uneasy as in the first half of Henry IV's reign: sometimes it was harmonious as during the short reign of Henry V, even though the final result was a grave deterioration in the national finances.

So there is no question of attempting to trace the measure of resistance to Henry V's constant demands for war subsidies. Taxes were paid throughout the reign with remarkable promptitude so that it was possible to keep faith with loan holders both great and small and under his determined leadership and immense personal prestige both Parliament and Convocation were generous and compliant. In fact the domestic history of the reign seems only a pale shadow of the glorious campaigns in France, and after Agincourt the nation was only too eager to identify itself with Henry's struggle for the united crown of the two countries. The fiscal history of the reign therefore recalls the successful years of Edward III and is a record mainly of Henry's demands and Parliament's acquiescence instead of the carping criticism which had characterised his father's régime.

Henry V's first parliament did not meet until May and although it renewed the customs duties, the first half of the subsidy which it voted was not collectable until later in the year. This, however, was mere mark-time financing and no fresh grants were made by Parliament in the spring of 1414. By autumn the probing expedition to France, which was to culminate in Agincourt, was being planned and the November Parliament, as an obvious war measure, voted a double tenth and a double fifteenth without hesitation, collection to be February 1415 and a year later: the Parliament of 1416, however, put back this second tenth and fifteenth to June 1416.

Later in the year a double tenth and fifteenth were again voted, three-quarters to be paid by February and the balance to be set against loans made to the Crown in the following November. This pattern of generosity continued until the end of the reign with a double tenth and fifteenth in 1417, one-and-a-third of a tenth and fifteenth, the only case of this fraction, in 1419 and the final tenth and fifteenth in 1421. The total was a remarkable seven-and-three-quarters tenths and fifteenths in some six years, excluding the fractions earmarked for loan repayments.

The efforts of the clergy were no less impressive. They began by voting two tenths in 1415, payment to be a year apart, but, following the lead of the laity, the first of the tenths was advanced to June 1416. There was another two tenths grant in 1416 but in this case payment was delayed on the original 1415 grants. The same sort of procedure attached to the two tenths granted in 1417. Desire to be generous was outrunning performance for the clergy were incurring the grave risk of impoverishing themselves by these double tenths, a position the York Convocation realised in that year by voting one tenth only. In 1419 only a half tenth was to be levied along with a tenth to be collected from 1417, and finally, in 1421, there was a simple grant of one tenth.

Jointly then, the contribution of lay and ecclesiastical taxpayers showed a remarkable contrast to the yield in the previous reign. It has been estimated that under the grants from Parliament and Convocation a grand total of £216,865 was raised between 1415 and 1416, although even this extraordinary amount could not cover the military expenditure of the succeeding year and the deficit had to be made up by loans both from the leading men of the realm and the clergy. The commissioners who had been authorised to accept loans told the people quite unreservedly and openly what they were expected to pay and the remarkable thing is that so many complied. Borrowing then tapered off for three years to be resumed again with some intensity in 1421 since that year Henry failed to approach Parliament. Quite apart from his comparatively willing taxpayers and lenders, Henry V was also fortunate in the amount of money he obtained by way of ransom and in his policy, successful to a large extent, of making Normandy pay for the war effort. His average annual income approximated to the best years of Richard II.

Inevitably there were some complaints. A contemporary historian commented "our lord the king, rending (i.e. taxing) every man through the realm be he rich or poor, designs to return again into France in full strength.... in truth the grievous taxation of the people to this end being unbearable, accompanied with murmurs and with smothered curses among them from hatred of the burden....". Parliament, too, on the broader issue of constitutional development took momentary alarm at the prospect of the King of England becoming also the King of France after the Treaty of Troyes: taxation by consent might have taken a very different turn if Henry V had survived to rule a new Anglo-French state from Paris.

Less and less was now being heard of the king "living of his own" which basically meant giving an example of good management in return for which parliament would not be ungenerous. The phrase had never implied asking the king to renounce taxation, and this was a manifest impossibility in a period of endemic warfare. It became increasingly convenient, therefore, for the king to raise the extra taxation needed for foreign campaigns not by individual bargains, as in the case of loans, but by meeting the representatives of the boroughs and shires in the Westminster Chapter House. For all the superficial amity however, the general picture of English government finance in the nine years of Henry V's reign is basically no happier than it had been during his father's, as the mediaeval hero-king pursued his quest, at once desperate and quixotic, for the obsolete ideal of Anglo-French unity.

There is nothing artificial in the treatment of taxation history reign by reign since the personality of the king was an all-important factor. The very active part taken by both Henry IV and Henry V in the financial affairs of the state underlines the considerable loss of momentum during the minority of Henry VI, when, in a period of peculiar difficulty and tension, government was by the royal Council which displayed an inevitable diversity of interests.

The Exchequer, however, again showed its ability to continue its complex financing techniques without any firm directive from the king, although there was an immediate drop in real revenue from which there was no recovery for some time and a sharp decline in the number of days business done at the Treasury. This contraction of activity was a direct result of Parliament's ability to curb both taxation and expenditure without the mailed hand and imperious personality of Henry V: for instance, only a grudging and ad hoc payment from the Customs of 13s. 4d. on every sack of wool and on every 240 tanned skins exported from Calais was ordered for defence purposes, the general rate of dues being reduced from 50s. 0d. to 40s. 0d. The second Parliament was no more generous, voting no additional taxation whatever. Fortunately customs proved buoyant even when scaled down and in 1427 contributed towards the highest total of real revenue for the next six years.

It was inevitable, therefore, that the government's need for loans should continue unabated and in the first credit drive of the reign Beaufort, the premier nobleman, provided over £9,000 out of a total of £12,000: his loans in fact were to reach a massive £45,000 in the first decade and, by the diversion of customs to his own use through the appointment of an agent in every port, he achieved for a time a virtual stranglehold on the national finances. The third and fourth Parliament of the reign, in 1425 and 1427 respectively, were of little immediate help, making only grants which were to be effective twelve months hence.

A strong monarch would have demanded more fiscal co-operation from the outset: even the Council was beginning to find the situation intolerable. In April 1428, therefore, the first grant of the reign was voted: its yield appears to have been small since the government had parliamentary encouragement to borrow simultaneously up to a limit of £24,000. The fifth Parliament, prompted no doubt by the current series of military disasters, symbolised by the tragic and moving story of Joan of Arc, was the first to make really generous grants, voting two subsidies payable at the beginning and end of 1430 as well as tunnage and poundage and the appropriate wool duties. The January Parliament of 1431 was equally generous but at somewhat longer range, voting a subsidy and a third, the whole to be paid in November 1431 and the third at Easter 1432. The May 1432 Parliament, however, must have regretted its predecessor's sudden burst of liberality, granting only a meagre half subsidy and that spread over sixteen months, in two instalments.

So in the first decade of the young king's minority the fiscal impetus of the preceding reign was virtually confined to existing taxes: any additional subsidies needed conciliar initiative. The real revenue averaged about £75,000 annually and there was a fall in borrowed money, which was just as well since the niggardliness of Parliament made it hard for the government to meet its obligations. The primary function of taxation was to guarantee as far as possible a steady cash flow by underwriting successive loans which enabled the administration of the country to be carried on.

In 1433 there was a change of Treasurer when Kynwolmerssh was succeeded by Cromwell. He proceeded to draw up a national balance-sheet, an exercise not recently essayed except in a very perfunctory fashion. Nicholas Dixon, an experienced Exchequer clerk, was responsible for the figures. Briefly, revenue was £36,000 of which some £27,000 was customs and excise, leaving a bare £9,000 as the ordinary Crown revenue. Annual expenditure was running at the rate of £58,000 and total debts were a seemingly astronomical £164,000. However, taking the revenue figure of £36,000 and the average yield of a lay tenth and fifteenth and a clerical tenth which was £44,000, the Exchequer could well congratulate itself on a surplus of £22,000, the difference between a gross income of £80,000 and the £58,000 expenses, which could be used for the liquidation of debts. In other words, and with the occasional assistance of a subsidy, a precarious solvency was possible. Without parliamentary goodwill, however, clearly any government could only stagger from one financial crisis to another, as long as the war continued. The problem here was the number of loan holders, great and small, who had a vested interested in its prolonging, although there was an increasingly vocal section who could see nothing in France, since the war had long since ceased to pay for itself, but increasing political bitterness and national bankruptcy.

It was the fact that current revenues were so heavily mortgaged in advance, coupled with the fact that England had now virtually lost the Hundred Years' War, which led to the fiscal experiment of 1436. Since the estimates of 1433, Parliament had granted two subsidies in the usual form, which was its normal way of coping with extra-ordinary pressures on finance, but a sort of income tax had been tried in 1404 and 1411 and although the rate averaged something less than

2 per cent, the yield had been gratifyingly large. In 1435 the time was ripe for a more comprehensive income tax as compared with the quota-based tax on moveables which had never been equitable and, since 1344, had been unresponsive to economic change.

This "subsidie" as the "trewe, pour Communes" termed it was, briefly, a graduated income tax. The minimum taxable income was £5 and the rate on the range from that figure to £100 was 6d. (2.5%). From £100 to £400 the rate was 8d. (3%) and from £400 upward a heavy 2s. 0d. (10%), the rate of the 1799 income tax. New assessments for this tax were necessary, and for this purpose the Council designated commissioners who should summon men whose incomes might prove to be taxable: but since these commissioners would be local men it was always possible to bring influence to bear on them for the trimming of such assessments. Four "tresorers and receyvours of the said subsidie" were appointed to administer the disbursement of the tax and to retain such wages and rewards as the king should decide and announce in Parliament. The yield was between £8,500 and £9,000, and this type of tax was to become the established form of grant under the Tudors and the first two Stuarts.

There is an interesting postscript to the income tax of 1435–36. An analysis of the returns seemed to show that the total taxable income of the baronage was less than a third of that which can be allocated to the knights, esquires and merchants. The suggested political implication of this would be that the Lords did not, in the mid-fifteenth century, dominate the Commons since the latter had, on that evidence, even stronger financial interests. Clearly, however, the method of assessment used could hardly inspire confidence as it was based only on sworn statements not on any verifiable figures, and some of the known incomes of the greater nobles were far in excess of their returns: for instance, Anne, Dowager Countess of Stafford, was assessed at £1,950, at least £500 short of her real income, and the first Duke of York at £3,320 when his income was more than double: even the Lord Treasurer himself, Cromwell, was assessed at £1,007 when his income was well in excess. Nor was it clear precisely what revenue was liable: freeholds, one of the subjects of charge, were not easy to define, and royal grants, held during pleasure, wardships and Welsh possessions were exempt. The next income tax was to be more comprehensive, but certainly large incomes were taxed more heavily than they had been in previous subsidies of this kind even if some sources escaped the net.

In 1437 Henry VI attained his majority but there was no dramatic change in the financial scene, except that nearly half the wool duty was allocated to the defence of Calais. If that was not discouraging enough the Parliament of 1438–1439 sullenly refused any new grants and in the Hilary term there were extensive sales of Crown lands. The 1439–1440 Parliament, however, was eventually rather more generous, granting a subsidy and a half for 1440 and 1441 together with the usual customs and a small poll tax on aliens which, with another subsidy, was continued until 1443. Cash receipts in the rolls varied from the magnificent windfall of the ransom of Charles, Duke of Orleans, to the carefully recorded penny, the net amount less charges and exemptions, from the Oxfordshire collectors in respect of the lay subsidy.

Such minutiae were symptomatic of the disastrous level to which revenue sank in 1443–1444. Even in the following year, Parliament insisted on keeping grants low just when they were most needed, authorising only a mere half-subsidy, and again, for the three years ending in 1448. Admittedly later grants of tunnage and poundage, and the wool duties for four years, injected new life, but the all-time low of the 1445–1446 period was underlined by the ironic noting of the insignificant sum of £2 as a donum, emphasising the limited extent to which the king could look for help from his loyal subjects. Parliament's half-subsidy of 1449, reduced by an abatement of £3,000 for the relief of "decayed towns", was reluctantly fully subsidised later in the year by a further half and the allocation of £10,000 against the expenses of the royal household. In addition, the ever-buoyant customs remained the firm financial standby of the Lancastrian dynasty, supplemented by some increase in the poll tax on aliens, and a prolongation of the wool duties.

In 1450, however, the formal resumption of the war by France, resulting in the loss of the whole of Normandy, forced a reconsideration of the whole financial position which had merely been patched-up by the grants of the previous summer. A statement of affairs was drawn up, echoing the balance-sheet exercise of 1433, which computed the royal debts at £372,000, in all likelihood an exaggerated figure, and the royal income at £5,000 which was a tactical error as it inevitably set the Commons off in pursuit of their favourite policy of resumption. In return for Henry's agreement an income tax was granted, broader based than had been the levy of 1435–36 and including this time, Welsh landlords. The rates were 6d. in the pound for incomes between £1 and £20, 1s. 0d. in the pound for incomes between £20 and £200, with 2s. 0d. in the pound being the subsequent rate. The grant was considered exceptional and the Commons prayed the king that it might not be taken in example hereafter, but as a thing granted for the defence of the realm, in the king's "most grettest necessite for they could not and dared not in any wise" grant the usual tenth and fifteenth; which gave rise to the awkward rumour that these were to be abolished; and, as collection was slow, the tax was no help for immediate financial exigencies. It is noteworthy that in the manifesto of grievances issued by Jack Cade at the time of the Kent uprising and three-day occupation of London in 1450, heavy taxation and the illegal appointment of collectors of taxes were important items of complaint, resulting in the beheading by the rebels of the Treasurer, Lord Saye & Sele. The tax was not a success: the commissioners had proved "lacking in diligence" and the persons chargeable showed a marked reluctance to attend for examination.

The next session of Parliament was not until 1453 and under the somewhat spasmodic Lancastrian influence quite generous grants were made, but by that time the king having been reduced to trading in alum and the selling of some of the Crown Jewels, the financial machine was barely ticking over, and real revenue had sunk to its nadir. Even the voting of a whole subsidy, the grant of tunnage and poundage for life at existing rates and of the wool duties at increased rates, could not satisfy the urgent need for ready cash; so much so that an offer to raise much-needed soldiers, the cost of which might well have amounted to three subsidies, had to be sacrificed for an immediate half-subsidy.

By now all new grants were being anticipated as soon as authorised, and 1455, the date of the first battle of St. Albans in which Henry VI was defeated by Yorkist forces, ushered in a disastrous decade. Real revenue was below £10,000 annually and the Yorkist Parliament of that year was the only one seriously to consider the financial situation. Customs remained the saving grace but even they, on occasions, could be seriously weakened, as for instance when the Duke of York, being in a position to do so, redeemed some of his loans by shipping a quantity of duty-free wool: in addition evasion of the duty and corruption of the officials became increasingly common. The Lancastrians had to subsist miserably on this diminishing income and Parliament, when they plucked-up enough courage to summon one, simply busied itself with Yorkist prosecutions. Meanwhile real revenue had sunk to the lowest figure of the reign, and this was not to recover until Edward IV had firmly established himself on the throne after his signal victory at Towton in 1461.

This summary of the financial dealings of the Lancastrian monarchy shows clearly that the income from all sources, tenths and fifteenths, customs and all the profit from royal lands was perennially insufficient to cover its commitments. A precarious solvency and an adequate day to day inflow of ready cash could only be achieved by an elaborate credit system. Indebtedness was a permanent feature of mediaeval finance and, as previously noted, grants of taxation were used not for liquidating current expenditure, since collection was invariably slow and grants often postdated, but as security for immediate cash advances in the form of assignments or anticipatory drafts on revenue. However, it was not always possible to honour these promises to pay and they would then be converted to fictitious loans which might be met, wholly or partly, in the next round of receipts.

This confused and confusing system was hardly conducive to royal creditworthiness and advances would have dried up had not there been valuable considerations for loans, the simplest being a promise to repay a sum greater than the extent of the actual cash loan. Certainly there were delays in repayment, but the Whittingtons and the Beauforts comfortably cushioned by their remaining capital, could afford to wait.

This cumbersome and elaborate system was held together and operated by the Exchequer. Too much should not be made of the independence of this body for the officials of the Upper Exchequer were terrified of admitting any claim for allowance without the fullest authority: they tried to safeguard themselves behind their bureaucratic procedures, a practice which has a modern ring. However, efficient or not, bureaucratic or not, the Exchequer did provide an invaluable element of administrative continuity, year after year, through dynastic ambitions, abdications, civil wars and foreign campaigns without any major change in personnel except at the top and with its executive techniques intact. Without it the creaking finances of the pauper Lancastrian government could never have survived.

There were also two other sources of revenue which contributed towards solvency. The first of these was the series of ecclesiastical grants, for both king and Council regarded the Convocations as an integral part of the country's fiscal machinery. The technique of the royal officials was to estimate the quantum of the Crown's needs and dispatch representative lords to the clerical assembly to urge this figure upon the clergy: if it was agreed, the process of collection could begin. In addition to the payment of tenths and half-tenths by the secular Church and the liable religious houses, after 1422 the device of a "charitable subsidy" was introduced, which charged both chaplains and pensioners, normally exempt, swelling the taxation from religious sources. Exempt monasteries, however, still retained their exemption and the fiscal policy of Convocation was also to exempt the poorer clergy.

Secondly, there was the policy of resumption which, as previously mentioned, had always been Parliament's panacea for royal pleas of financial malaise, and certainly in the disastrous last stages of the Hundred Years' War there had been wholesale dissipation of royal lands and resources. Parliament, however, never claimed that resumption was a substitute for taxation but simply that it would lessen the Crown's claims on parliamentary grants.

In 1450 the Act of Resumption was passed with 186 provisos of exemption for members of the government and their supporters. The second Act of 1451, however, had only 43 such provisos, excluding all the previous exemptions unless specifically re-enacted. Income from the resumed lands now became sound backing for assignments and, more important, the king acquired a valid claim on Parliament's generosity to the extent that resumptions proved insufficient. In fact, the Parliament of 1453 turned out to be the most lavish of the reign and resumption continued to be, as late as 1455, the royal road to parliamentary co-operation.

With the accession of Edward IV not only was there a successful pursuit of the Lancastrian policy of resumption but also a significant revival in the importance of the monarch himself. The 1461 Parliament, a very full assembly, had unequivocally proclaimed him "the very true and rightful heir to the throne", but even so, with Warwick the Kingmaker in the background, the king had to move cautiously. He asked for no grants and his first problem was whether he could provide adequate recompense to his supporters from the resumptions and confiscations. He was, however, voted customs for life, although at reduced rates; but an increased volume of trade in the latter half of the reign more than made up the initial deficiency.

The Parliament of 1463 was the first to make a grant, earmarked for defence only. Basically it was the traditional tenth and fifteenth of £37,000 gross but there were complications. £6,000 of this, the usual shortfall on account of wasteland, was to be raised in the form of a tax on moveables and the balance in the usual way. In addition assessment and collection were to be controlled by royal officials. This attempted innovation failed. Edward remitted the £6,000 and the residue was ordered to be paid under the general form of a fifteenth "heretofore used and accustomed". The Convocations were more forthcoming yielding two-and-a-half tenths, as well as a "charitable subsidy" from Canterbury and a tenth from York.

At the opening of his Parliament of 1467, Edward declared "The cause why I have summoned and called my present parliament is that I purpose to live upon mine own and not to charge my subjects but in great and urgent causes"; and although there were further resumptions, it was not until it assembled again in the following year that two subsidies were voted and a clerical tenth by Convocation, both grants being on the pretext of resuming the French war. Before long, however, the danger of acute civil war fomented by France and Warwick loomed, not to be dissipated finally until the battles of Barnet and Tewkesbury.

In 1472 Edward recommenced his anti-French diplomacy which involved him again in complicated fiscal arrangements with Parliament. Briefly, the grant initially made had only produced a little over £31,000, partly because some of the northern counties had failed to pay. The Commons therefore ordered the defaulters to pay £5,383, the cost of a year's wages for 590 archers at 6 pence per day, and regranted the 1473 subsidy which had not been collected. The aim was to provide the annual wages of 13,000 archers: the difference between that sum and the estimated yield of the subsidy and the fine, some £51,000, was to be raised by a special tax, assessable on goods and chattels in the first instance, but should this levy fail to attain the whole sum specified in the commission, the royal commissioners were empowered in the lengthy and elaborate provisions of the Act, to charge the deficiency "on the lands and rents and other possessions of freehold".

These changes in assessment and collection not surprisingly proved "so diffuse and laborious" that the tax never really got off the ground, quite apart from widespread peculation by the collecting staff. Parliament, therefore, on the ground that "the most easy, ready and prone payment" was by the grant of fifteenths and tenths, prayed the king to remit the said sum of £51,000 and take one-and-three-quarters of a whole fifteenth and tenth "the sums whereof exceed the aforesaid sum to be taken "in maner and fourme aforetyme used". One significant point should finally be noted: although the net result of Edward's projected fiscal reforms was the retention of the old tenth-fifteenth nexus, royal commissioners were now being employed to a greater extent than the local administration, that is, collection was becoming centralised.

Edward's tortuous negotiations with France finally secured him the grant of a considerable pension of 50,000 gold crowns as well as a 75,000 crown initial payment. He was graciously pleased to remit part of the war grant and began to concentrate on building up his own private fortune. He had always been a man of business and his estate management, when Earl of March, reflected his close attention to financial detail. Then, as a contemporary chronicler put it, "He turned all his thoughts to the question how he might in future amass an amount of treasure worthy of his royal station out of his own substance, and by the exercise of his own energies.... He assumed possession of nearly all the royal estates. Throughout all the parts of the kingdom he appointed inspectors of the customs, men of remarkable shrewdness but too hard, according to general report, upon the merchants. The king himself, also, having procured merchant ships, put on board of them the finest wools, cloths, tin and other products of the kingdom and, like a private individual living by trade, exchanged merchandise for merchandise." He also traded on his popularity by extracting benevolences sometimes by individual application to the rich, sometimes by means of commissioners. His personal approach relied heavily on his peculiar brand of regal charisma. One documented story concerns the wealthy widow who gave the king £20 saying it was for his "lovely countenance". The king, who had "looked for scarce half that sum, thanked her and lovingly kissed her" whereupon she doubled the benevolence either, as the chronicler ingenuously surmises, "because she esteemed the kiss of the king so precious a jewel" or "because the flavour of his breath did so comfort her stomach".

Behind such trifles of fiscal history and the way "he slyde lyttle by lyttle into avarice", Edward was busy making his Chamber both a centre of audit and a treasury, imposing new standards of economy and solvency on his royal demesne through his own receivers, surveyors and accountants of land revenues. The Chamber had always been important: it was now becoming a fiscal cabinet and by the time of Henry VII it had superseded the Exchequer of Receipt. Only one Parliament was summoned between 1475 and 1483: this granted a tenth and a fifteenth and a poll tax on aliens. Despite the flurry of tentative fiscal reforms, customs still remained the most lucrative source of ready cash and the best security for loans from officials and powerful traders. Ironically enough the Lancastrian ideal of a full Treasury, resumptions, a co-operative Parliament and efficient kingship were only realised by the rival Yorkists.

The brief reigns of Edward V and Richard III were a melancholy coda to the regime of Edward IV. The one Parliament of the latter period simply made the now traditional grant of customs dues for life and enacted a statute against benevolences which Richard would approve as a popular move to prop his shaky title. However, the survival of a pocket-book of the king's signet clearly reveals that administratively there was a continuation of governmental policies and practices which the strong personality and fiscal acumen of Henry VII was to turn to good account.

The fifteenth century, then, should not be regarded as a period when civil strife and financial disorder culminated in a situation so desperate that the Tudors had to start rebuilding from the foundations. Rather it was a time of intense administrative development, the so-called Wars of the Roses being dynastic struggles among the magnates to whom the king was primus inter pares, not rebellion on a national scale. From the financial standpoint the fifteenth century was equally significant. Despite reliance on customs it saw the first graduated income tax as well as an embryo land tax and although these experiments proved unsuccessful, they were indicative of the resilience of a fiscal organisation long used to coping with an elaborate credit network. The frequent Lancastrian Parliaments were proof not of constitutional advance but financial stringency, and the less frequent Yorkist Parliaments were conditioned not by royal manipulation but by the fact that Edward IV deliberately devised a revenue system increasingly independent of parliamentary grants. The annual average of parliamentary levies enjoyed by Henry V and Henry VI was more than twice that of Edward IV despite Parliament's general compliance with his taxation demands, but he took the view that if he could economise on direct taxation he could equally economise on parliamentary sessions and so spare the poor, true Commons. Such a policy was equally attractive to the Commons themselves and there were no contemporary constitutionalists to warn them of the dangers ahead.

Chapter V

Tudor Housekeeping

The year 1485 was long regarded as the watershed between the mediaeval and the modern, just as Henry VII himself was hailed as the first of the representative monarchs in this renaissance. In fact, the same dangers menaced the first of the Tudors as had the last of the Yorkists, overmighty subjects, social unrest, pestilence, agricultural depression, declining trade and spiritual malaise, and Henry tended to look to the past for his remedies especially as he had grown-up in exile and held only theoretical knowledge of English governmental practice. The only real novelty was that of a native dynasty, the first since 1066 and the last before the twentieth century.

In the process of restoring the power of the central government no factor was more vital than finance. Henry had entered upon a sadly diminished inheritance: he was a poor man himself, heavily in debt to his backers in France and Brittany who had financed his invasion enterprise. These creditors he scrupulously repaid, thus establishing a useful creditworthiness: this was combined with the reintroduction of careful personal management by Henry himself, and controlled spending such as had not been seen since the early days of Edward IV. As far as fiscal techniques went, he had the option of concentrating on varieties of direct taxation, striving to increase the customs yield, or applying the policy of resumption coupled with reformed administration. In the event he experimented with all three courses.

The only institution capable of producing additional revenue legitimately was Parliament, and although the greater proportion of royal expenditure was now no longer personal, the land-owners who dominated Parliament were reluctant to share the cost of government except in emergency, a sentiment which coincided with Henry Tudor's own regard for tradition and political expediency. Hence the story of his seven Parliaments is, superficially, the story of sessions called for funding a series of military campaigns.

The battle of Stoke, in 1487, generally taken as the last battle in the Roses' war, was the first example. Parliament readily granted two tenths and fifteenths to cover the cost which Henry supplemented with heavy fines on the vanquished. Two years later, in 1489, came the first directly assessed subsidy of the Tudor period. There had only been seven such grants before 1485: in general they were unsuccessful, not to be regarded as precedents, and Parliament's suspicious and hostile attitude was underlined in its attempts to retain control of their yield. The occasion was the expedition to assist the Duke of Brittany and the grant was the pay of 10,000 archers for the year, £100,000, £75,000 of which was to come from the laity and £25,000 from the clergy. Again, it was "not to be taken for example or precedent" and no information on details of assessments or even amounts due from any area were to be released to the Exchequer.

The levy was administered by commissioners who were not, as with the tenth and fifteenth, mere collectors: they in fact made the assessments "after their discretion," and appointed collectors who should be "able and sufficient" inhabitants of the area. The rate was a tenth of annual income from all freeholders as from 1 January 1489 after deduction of "all rents, fees and services" coupled with a tax on moveables. Personal possessions were, however, exempt as were ships using the sea and their tackle. Individuals were assessable in the place "where they were most conversant".

The upshot was bitterly disappointing in two vital aspects. Its unpopularity in Yorkshire and Durham sparked off an uprising and, when the Earl of Northumberland attempted to implement the functions of the commissioners in a "harsh and vexatious manner", his house was attacked and he himself slain. The yield, too, was disconcertingly low at a maximum of £27,000 not even the yield of the standardised tenth and fifteenth. Contemporary opinion blamed the costs of collection and the bias of the commissioners to their neighbours, and both the degree of failure and the means of rectification harked back to the earlier fifteenth century subsidies, for the king remitted the deficiency on receiving the grant of a tenth and fifteenth in 1490.

For the expedition to France, Henry took in 1491 a benevolence from the more wealthy with the quasi-parliamentary authority of the

Great Council, as well as the usual tenths and fifteenths. The commissioners were instructed by Chancellor Morton to act on the principle that "such as are sparing in their manner of living must have
saved money while those that live in a splendid manner give evidence
of ability to pay" – the notorious Morton's fork or the fifteenth
century version of Catch 22. In the event, although as Dudley said
"War is a marvellous consumer of treasure and riches", Henry
showed a profit on this campaign and emerged also with a pension of
50,000 francs.

Before the end of the reign there were two more experiments in
direct taxation. In 1497 the target was £120,000 specifically for the
Scottish campaign to be raised by two tenths and fifteenths, £60,000,
and a subsidy of the same amount. This represented a hybridisation
of the traditional fixed yield levy and the growing tendency to assess
according to wealth. Administratively this levy was the same as the
1489 subsidy except for the restriction of liability to lands and
tenements, fees and offices being omitted. The whole subsidy was
conditional on the Crown's execution of the full military expedition
promised in the preamble to the Act and the lump sum of £60,000 was
never in fact levied. It was just as well since Cornwall had already
risen against the tax on the ingenious grounds that for an expedition
to Scotland scutage was the constitutional form of levy. Not that
Henry was dissatisfied with only half the amount originally legislated
for, since even at £60,000 he had a tolerable credit balance. The
subsidy of 1504, however, £30,000, was a reversion to the tenth and
fifteenth formula even to the amount.

In some ways Henry was able to afford his experiments with
direct taxation since he could rely, throughout his reign, on a steadily
increasing revenue from customs. He had been given the usual life-
grant on his accession of the duties on wool, skins and leather:
tunnage and poundage followed in 1490 by the addition of a special
duty on malmsey, still popular despite the unhappy fate of the Duke of
Clarence, imported from Crete. His reforms here were not administrative but mainly in the direction of encouraging trade. He began in
1487 by banning coastal trade without certification. Then followed a
series of commercial treaties with the Netherlands, Denmark, France,
Spain and Florence: the policy was to combine with the abolition of
foreign exemptions the promotion of good commercial relations. The
increased yield which followed automatically from expanding trade
was accelerated in 1507 by increased tariffs. The policy generally was
an unqualified success: in the first decade of the reign customs and

allied duties averaged some £33,000: in the second decade this rose to an average of over £41,000.

In his attempts to gain full credit for what he considered to be his just dues and demands, Henry stretched his financial prerogatives to the limit. He exploited justice with excessive fines and he even exacted feudal dues from all men with the requisite qualification of over £40 capital by insisting that they should assume knighthood. He demanded contributions, in 1504, for the knighting of his son Arthur, although, a macabre touch, that son had died in 1502, and he forced the appropriate dues for the marriage of his eldest daughter. However, this revival, as with his management of the temporalities of abbots and bishops, of the feudal nexus was not for the old traditional reasons but for solid financial gain: the revival was facilitated by the investigations to consider liability to feudal incidents, which were a vital part of recording a tenure shaken by civil war.

Henry VII's insistence on his feudal dues was partly for fiscal reasons and partly to consolidate his hold on the Crown and his rights as feudal overlord. His ordered acts of resumption of Crown lands were directed to the same end. The extent of resumptions, however, was not eroded by dynastic obligations: there was a complete dearth of members of the royal family who could absorb lands, and so carefully did Henry husband his resources, not indeed in the shape of agricultural improvements but by concentrating on every perquisite of office, that the yield from the royal demesne rose from less than £10,000 at the start of the reign to over £40,000 at the end, matching or even exceeding the yield of the customs and making a vital and calculable contribution to Tudor revenues.

The catalyst in all these financial developments was the royal household, which gradually displaced the Exchequer during the period. This replacement was not a steady process: indeed during the early years of Henry VII's reign the Exchequer was patiently and systematically regaining the audit ground it has lost under the later Yorkists. It was some time before the king judged the time was ripe for sustaining a takeover bid for the antique Exchequer machinery in favour of the more streamlined methods of the royal household by which the Treasurer of the Chamber became the chief financial officer of the Crown. This finally depended on the king's own supreme concentration on the health of his revenues, which even included the personal annotating of account books and the personal exoneration of his accountants from Exchequer processes.

Yet there were no real reforms or innovations. Direct taxation was still dependent on the fixed quota of the tenth and fifteenth since local partiality had made attempts at a tax on income innocuous. Indirect taxation certainly had increased with the expansion of trade but smuggling and the underpaid customs service led to evasion and corruption. Benevolences and feudal incidents were the survivors of a system of financing which had lost reality, and needed the ferocious supervision of an Empsom or a Dudley. Land revenues were better administered without the lands themselves being better cultivated. So although Henry did succeed in his last few years in attaining the mediaeval fiscal target of living of his own, it is arguable that he could have further consolidated the royal finances instead of simply replacing the old assignment system with a straight cash system plus a bullion reserve, the "felicity of full coffers" as Bacon put it. At the same time Henry also began to show the same blend of avarice and superstition which characterised Louis XI, but by then the fiscal triumph of bringing four-fifths of the country's revenue under his personal control was being menaced by its inability to absorb any abnormal expenditure such as war. In addition, from the beginning of the century, there had been a continuous fall in the value of money resulting from the influx of precious metals from the Americas: merchants and manufacturers increased their prices: wages rose: but fixed incomes from land felt the result of the inflation, a condition not unknown today. Finally Henry's financial policy created amongst the peerage a fear of the looming danger of authoritarian government.

The general outline of fiscal history during the reign of Henry VIII is deceptively simple. It starts with the arraignment of Empsom and Dudley for treason, and their execution can be taken as symbolic of the break with the régime of the first Tudor together with the dissipation of what ready money was available on such exercises in regal grandeur as the Field of Cloth of Gold. Then followed the period of Wolsey's supremacy whose oppressive taxation policy made enemies of those whose hostility finally caused his downfall. Thomas Cromwell retrieved the situation partly by more efficient management and partly by the expropriation and sale of monastic lands. However, in the end, to pursue his futile and ill-conducted wars, the king destroyed the financial independence of the Crown and undermined the prosperity of the country.

Such a précis has a considerable measure of justification just as Henry himself has a good deal to answer for. The old economy had gone and the new king had neither the same interest or the same expertise in financial matters as his father. Thus a delegation of fiscal responsibility to ministers, however able, only intensified the problem of how to fund the hostility engendered by his divorce proceedings in particular and his aggressive foreign policy in general: in fact his resources were strained to breaking point especially as some important sources of revenue showed a decline quite apart from the depression of incomes caused by inflation.

The first casualty was customs. In the last year of Henry VII's reign the yield had exceeded £42,000: in the last year of Henry VIII's reign, 1547, this had fallen to less than £35,000 despite the debasement of the currency. The reasons were not far to seek. The export of raw wool had declined from 8,469 sacks in 1509–1510 to about 4,700 in 1546–1547, due to his aggressive foreign policy, but the export of manufactured woollen cloth and articles which paid tunnage and poundage had increased considerably. This all-round expansion of trade, however, was not reflected in the returns because the imposts on cloth were relatively light while those on wool were heavy. The yield of tunnage and poundage was computed on the government's Book of Rates, based on 1507 valuations: clearly, without an updating of the Book of Rates, as currency devaluation continued, the income from this source would diminish in real terms unless there happened to be a spectacular advance in trade. In addition there was the ever-present problem of corruption: the collectors and their entourage of minor officials were ill paid and thus susceptible to bribery. In general however, the fall in customs yield signified not a decline in the export market but a redistribution.

Henry, like his father, also attempted to multiply his income by reviving feudal practices such as insisting on knighthood or exploiting the clergy by imposing fines for real or trumped up charges. In 1532 began the long battle for the Statute of Dues, designed to confirm the royal rights on a tenant's death and to prevent evasion of just and due payments, but this amounted to no more than a temporary expedient and failed to solve the lasting problem of a static revenue in an age of rising cost.

There were no changes in the organisation of the royal estates apart from the fact that, since Henry had not the fervent personal interest of his father in finance generally, not even in this source of revenue which had become the major contributor to the royal purse, Parliament appointed two general surveyors of Crown lands to administer the income from these properties, and incidentally to audit other revenue accounts. This system worked well, but even so, and with the minimum of alienation, real income fell steadily before the erosion of inflation and currency debasement in the latter part of the reign. It was vital, therefore, that some untapped source of supply to exploit should be discovered.

The dissolution of the monasteries is relevant in the context of fiscal history only to the extent that the inflow of new capital and revenue relieved the pressure on orthodox and traditional forms of taxation. Diversions of ecclesiastical wealth, whether in the form of ecclesiastical levies, such as the clerical tenths, or straight expropriations, as in the case of the Knights Templar, were no new feature in English financial policy. Now this process was to crystallise on a wholesale scale and with frightening speed, parallel with similar movements on the Continent.

The exigencies of the divorce proceedings, the secular drive of Thomas Cromwell and the waning popularity of the orders all contributed to the downfall of monasticism, but the prime motive for the attack was the property of the Church, variously estimated at one-fifth to one-third of all the land in the country. The first move was the transfer to the Crown of the payment of first-fruits and tenths, calculated to bring in some £40,000 annually. Early in the following year, 1535, commissions were issued for the valuation of all ecclesiastical property in England: the report was amazingly accurate even by modern standards and proved a detailed springboard from which Cromwell could mount his first attack. The first series of visitations resulted in the closure of the smaller establishments. The Pilgrimage of Grace was the precursor and, to an extent, the excuse for the completion of the process. By 1539 the larger monasteries had been suppressed and a minor revolution accomplished with both ease and thoroughness.

From a financial point of view the operation was a complete success since what Henry and Cromwell had wanted in the first place was a large sum of ready money: any permanent increase in income was a secondary consideration. In the period between 1536 and 1538 the Crown sold lands to the value of nearly £30,000 and goods to the value of £7,000, retaining rents with an annual value of over £27,000. Admittedly the gap between income and expenditure was still not closed, but a land-owning class was now so firmly committed to the fact of Reformation by lavish purchases of monastic land that it was impossible for Mary to pursue any policy of resumption and the Crown retained its incidental accretion of income. What the revival of feudal exactions had been to Henry VII, the monasteries were to his son.

On the debit side, therefore, Henry had to reckon with a decline in customs and in feudal dues and although the income from the royal estates was vastly improved by the injection of monastic rents, his lack of personal surveillance and the insidious effect of inflation left his budget still unbalanced. Happily, there were two important items on the credit side.

The first asset was continuity in administration. Sir John Heron continued as Treasurer of the Chamber until his death in 1524: his successors were two experienced Treasury knights, Sir Henry Wyatt until 1528 and then, a long stint, Sir Brian Juke to 1545. Apart from the appointment of the two surveyors of Crown lands, the administrative machine was virtually unchanged until the advent of Thomas Cromwell. Some changes were forced upon him, as, for instance, the new department for dealing with ecclesiastical revenues, but eventually he set up six departments of state, each staffed with its own officials and responsible for specified types of revenue. Inevitably there was a certain amount of overlapping but the excessive formality of the old Exchequer was avoided on the one hand, and the casual accounting of the household on the other; that is as long as Cromwell's strong guiding hand was present to direct and control.

Secondly, there was a most important fiscal innovation developed by this financial secretariat. It is clear from the history of direct taxation to the death of Henry VII that experiments to replace the tenth and fifteenth by the subsidy had failed. Parliament apparently preferred the older form of taxation to any other: it was a readily intelligible tax, hallowed by tradition and of fixed yield, apart from an occasional variance in the deduction for ruin and decay. The collection procedure was standardised and control directly exercised by Parliament. It could, however, pose problems: there were negligent or fraudulent officials which was not surprising when their poundage was only 1 per cent: the office itself was unpopular, ground between the upper millstone of local resentment and the lower of the inexorable pressure from the Exchequer: and there were built-in complexities of exemption and distraint for non-payment. In all it was an elaborate procedure for gathering a gross figure of only £37,000, considering the contemporary value of money. Admittedly its predictability was an advantage, it avoided any inquisition and its incidence was left to local discretion, but it was unfairly distributed and the need to devise an alternative and more elastic tax was self-evident.

The obvious course, however unpromising, was to capitalise on the experience of the previous directly assessed subsidies of which there had been seven prior to the Tudors and four in the reign of Henry VII. Although these had been disappointing in yield and suspect by the Commons, they had left behind them a basis of administration by commissioners, the genesis of a tradition of impartiality even in face of the immediate interests of themselves, their friends and neighbours and a considerable extension of the subjects of charge.

In the event the final form of the directly assessed subsidy was attained in a comparatively short space of time: the four subsidies of 1513, 1514, 1515 and 1516 contained practically the whole process of evolution, and after the consolidation of 1523 formed the framework of a tax which lasted well into the seventeenth century.

The 1513 Act was the blueprint for the future. It combined with a poll tax of 4d. on everyone over fifteen, a graduated levy of 1s. 0d. where income was between £2 and £10, 1s. 8d. between £10 and £20 and 3s. 4d. between £20 and £40, and so on. It is noteworthy that wage-earners were included within its scope. A standard procedure was laid down for assessment and collection. Individual assessments were made by local officers on inhabitants, in writing, under the supervision of commissioners appointed nationally by Parliament, but later by the king. The numbers of these commissioners were increased from ten for each shire to thirty-five: in addition they had far wider powers of discretion and summary jurisdiction. There was a two-tier collection service, local or 'petty' collectors appointed by the commissioners and regionalised or 'high' collectors. The whole represented the first major extension of the incidence of taxation since 1380, the year of the first poll tax.

The three following subsidies of the three subsequent years showed further experimentation. In 1514 there was a named sum of £160,000 to be raised; but it is not clear how this amount was arrived at without any national survey of wealth. Greater precision was required here since the assessments were to the nearest pound. The target was clearly overambitious, the yield on both years being less than £50,000, which did not deter the government from aiming at the same sum in the following year, 1515, with an added proviso that the shortfall, if any, should be divided between the counties and boroughs. In 1516 there were minor modifications for a yield again below £50,000.

No Parliament met between 1515 and 1522 when the second French war necessitated the raising of unprecedented revenue between 1522 and 1524. In 1522 there was an ecclesiastical grant of half the spiritual revenues and a demand for a fifth of lay goods and land in face of which the Commons asked for "a more easier sum". Then followed the subsidy of 1523 for which Wolsey had demanded a 4s. 0d. rate, but although he was eventually granted four subsidies the overall rate was considerably scaled down: this 1523 Act virtually set the pattern for all subsequent subsidies. The immediate importance of this stabilisation was, however, overshadowed by the ironically so-called Amicable Grant of 1524, an arbitrary forced loan of one-sixth capital from the laity and one-third from the clergy, which has been termed the most violent financial transaction in English history, putting any currently proposed wealth tax in the shade. The unhappy collectors were still struggling with the returns from the two previous years when this new burden was thrust upon them. Recalcitrance was turning to rebellion until Henry personally intervened to remit the demands.

The history of parliamentary taxation from 1485 to 1547 is the history of a successful attempt to replace the fifteenth and tenth which was fixed, by a flexible directly assessed subsidy. The importance of the tenths and fifteenths had clearly begun to wane, in that after 1512 they were never granted without a subsidy and in the case of about half the subsidies authorised they were never granted at all. Henry still used the detested procedures of the benevolence and the forced loan, especially between 1540 and 1547, the period of the French and Scots wars, when his need for money ran highest. In 1542, for example, Parliament sanctioned his release from a forced loan of no less than £112,000, converting it into a permanent payment on account. Included in the subsidies also were the graduated poll taxes on aliens.

From 1523 the form of the subsidy settled down, apart from 1534 where the vague and imprecise drafting contrasted sharply with the skill of John Hales of Gray's Inn who had been responsible for the definitive Acts, for which he was paid £10. All assessments were made according to current values and everyone was to be taxed where they were "most conversant, abiding or recent" with penalties against fraudulent removal. These assessments were drafted by assessors, their preliminary figures then being accepted or altered by the commissioners: none of the assessors' preliminary certificates has survived so the extent of the revision remains unknown. Collection costs were about 6d. in the pound and the cash tended to come in slowly, the total charge taking about twelve months to complete. Complaints were few but abuses perhaps not so rare. Cromwell, in 1535, complained of "the deceit of the king in his subsidy" and seriously considered promulgating a new Act with fresh assessments. He settled for reassessing the City of London himself and multiplied the assessments certified by the commissioners by a penal two-and-a-half times. Then there was the case of Sir Anthony Cope of Oxfordshire, himself a commissioner, who deliberately omitted his own name from the lists of those liable to tax. He was eventually assessed on his own declaration but the duty due was doubled by way of a fine.

Despite these inevitable problems, the steady establishment of the fiscal validity of the subsidy under the second Tudor contrasts vividly with its hostile reception in the reign of Henry VII. This was peculiarly the work of Henry VIII for which he has been given far too little credit. His motive may have been his desperate need for more cash, but in some ways that only underlined his achievement.

From a fiscal standpoint, no clear pattern emerged in what might be called the interregnum of Edward VI and Mary, between the two great Tudors. The failure of Northumberland to balance the boy king's finances was to an extent set off under Mary by the appointment of the Marquis of Winchester as Lord Treasurer, the revision of the Book of Rates, the continuation of direct taxation, although by no means on a lavish scale, and the sensible amalgamation of the various revenue courts set up by Cromwell. These later developments, however, did not have time to take full effect, so that when Elizabeth came to the throne the Treasury was empty, the rearmament programme had halted and the government was in debt, partly to foreign bankers, to the extent of over £.25 millions, and subject to a "biting" interest: 25 per cent was not unusual.

The Elizabethan age was as great as it was fascinating. Every facet of rational thought and culture took on an aspect which even now looms larger than life. The '*Voyages*' of Hakluyt, the poetry of Sidney and Spenser, the plays of Shakespeare, a genius among others greatly gifted, the flourishing of architecture, music and science, all were united under a queen whose volatile personality inspired its visions and shaped its destiny. Exploration, commerce and agriculture developed and prospered, and the defeat of the Armada bore witness that England was once more a power in Europe.

Historians rightly emphasise the pageantry, the patriotism, the heroism of Elizabethan England, but behind the glamour and the adventure lay a patchwork financial system. Apart from customs and excise to a limited extent, this completely failed to tap the new wealth of the rising gentry and middle-classes. At the hint of any abnormal expenditure through an offensive or defensive foreign policy, the Crown had to go cap in hand to Parliament. Even so, the queen, throughout her reign, was found to exercise a parsimonious vigilance, with the assistance of an inadequate and venal civil service, and to eke out her revenue with such expedients as the sales of land or the profits of privateering. All this does not tarnish the glory of the era: rather it adds almost another dimension of wonder to the accomplishments of the first Elizabethans.

Elizabeth was fortunate on her accession to inherit as Lord Treasurer the Marquis of Winchester who had striven hard to restore order out of financial chaos after Henry VIII's military recklessness, the greed of Edward VI's advisers and the disappointments of Mary's reign. It was essential to increase the government's revenues and indeed this problem had been under active discussion before the death of Mary by several conciliar committees. As far as the royal demesne and the Crown lands were concerned a considerable programme of rationalisation had already been carried out. This led to a marked saving in administrative costs and more careful attention to exacting full manorial dues, but there was no attempt to bring rents up to their economic levels which would have been far more profitable, even when there were not long term. The consolidation of royal control over the landed estates was extended to the episcopal property which the new queen took over. The Crown consolidated by switching onerous and scattered livings for rich and productive estates.

Elizabeth's land revenues are relevant to her fiscal policy to the extent that the greater their contribution the less reliance needed to be placed on direct and indirect taxation. It has been calculated that the clear net yield of the Crown estates in the first year of Elizabeth's reign was £66,448. In the last year of her reign the figures were £88,767, a net increase of £22,319. The increase barely took care of the rate of inflation during the reign and could have been increased significantly had not Elizabeth fallen back on the old policies of her father who is reckoned to have sold some seven-eighths of the monastic land, and in her turn disposed of property to the annual rental value of £24,808, the sale of which yielded £813,332 to the Crown. That the net rental over the period increased was partly due to the confiscations and seizures from a still occasionally errant nobility as well as more efficient administration and further revenue secured from the Duchy of Lancaster and the Court of Wards which was set up in 1540 to administer the royal rights in wardships and marriages. But clearly the cherished ideal of regal self-sufficiency was barely tenable even in the earliest and most peaceful years of the reign.

Fortunately customs and excise showed a rapid and almost continuous increase throughout the period, Elizabeth reaping, to begin with, the benefits of Mary's revision of the Book of Rates in 1558 which raised the older rates by an average of approximately 75 per cent and switched the tax on wool to a tax on cloth. In the first year of her reign the duties amounted to nearly £83,000, the old customs yielding some £26,000 and the new tax on cloth alone almost reaching that figure. However, three factors militated against the government sitting back and simply enjoying the fruits of expanding trade and rising prices.

The first was the supervision exercised by the Exchequer over the accounting system of the customs whereby customs officials had to maintain individual and elaborate records for audit purposes. The Exchequer looked with suspicion on any attempt to introduce integration as an infringement of their traditional procedures. Winchester, however, went further than this. It was his intention to apply to the customs service the general surveyor, a Crown official who had been used with great success for the management of Crown estates; and he had already appointed Sir Francis Englefield to control the customs and collectors of London. He than proceeded to appoint deputy collectors "in creeks and havens" where the royal writ had not previously run: he issued a book of instructions in 1564 to improve the efficiency of collection, and a year later the Port Books which recorded the entries and clearances of goods from all English ports were instituted. This infrastructure was, when in full working order, to be crowned by the imposition of surveyors on a national scale, dealing with single commodities.

That this reform did not succeed was in the main due to the second factor, corruption and evasion. The creeks and havens which Winchester had tried to oversee were full of small craft smuggling goods in and out with the connivance of the collectors. This could be on a considerable scale. A commission searching in the Exeter customs regarding the import of wines during 1575–6 found that there were "in all landed 275 tons whereof entered, as by note appeareth, 77 tons: and so remaineth unentered 200, save two". The appointment of surveyors nation-wide would have acted as a grave deterrent to this flourishing trade in contraband, and since they were disliked by the Exchequer for impinging on its traditional functions and by the traders with a vital interest in illicit dealing, their services were quietly dispensed with in 1568.

Customs revenue was too valuable a component of national revenue to be abandoned either to the dead hand of Exchequer auditing procedures or the rapacity of evasion experts, however. Burghley had long considered that certainty of revenue should be the target, not the unrealistic aim, of the total dues to which the queen 'should be justly and truly answered'. There had been experiments of varying success in farming the dues on wine and cloth despite Winchester's opposition. What was now needed was a man of proven

administrative ability with customs experience and sufficient capital
to frank his bid for the farm. These criteria were fulfilled in the
legendary figure of Mr. Customer Smythe, a collector of tunnage and
poundage since the days of Queen Mary and married to the heiress of
one of the great Elizabethen merchant princes, Sir Andrew Judde.

He began by exploiting the Earl of Leicester's farm of sweet
wines and, in view of his success, Burghley turned over to him the
imposition on French wines generally in London. In 1570 Smythe
offered to pay for the import duties at London and its subsidiary ports
a rent of some £17,500 and a 'fine' of £5,000. Having invested this
immense sum, he took care to secure a proper return by using the
expertise he had gained as a collector, by increasing the efficiency of
the service and paying increased wages to officers of better quality.
Customs revenue increased steadily under his management and the
government tried to cream off the excess by negotiating ever larger
rents at the renewal dates. His last farm from 1584–1588 cost him
£30,000 but even so he turned in a net profit of £16,000. Eventually
Burghley tried to fix a rent at which even Smythe jibbed: perhaps it
was just as well since the government desperately needed every penny
to combat the Armada. The general surveyor system was accordingly
reintroduced but, although it did not survive the death of Burghley,
this experiment in farming customs could clearly be resorted to again,
since it had improved both efficiency of management and standards of
honesty.

Direct taxation still reflected the political situation far more
closely than indirect because it was still regarded as extraordinary, to
be resorted to only in periods of crisis. There were no innovations
during the reign: the pattern laid down by Henry VIII was sedulously
followed. Grants were made in thirteen parliamentary sessions and
up to 1587 the normal was two tenths and fifteenths and one subsidy.
From 1589 the menace of Spain and the expense of Ireland forced
Parliament into triple and even quadruple tenths and fifteenths: there
was only one year when less than £50,000 was collected from the laity:
and there were six years when the yield was over £100,000.

The revenue from one tenth and fifteenth had long been standardised: that from a subsidy usually reached £100,000, and a clerical
subsidy at 4s. 0d. was reckoned at £20,000. The rates applied to the
subsidy were 4s. 0d. of the annual value of land over £1 and 2s. 8d. of
the value of goods over £3. There were attempts towards the end of the
period when the pressure of taxes had become really onerous either
"to spare the £3 man" which was Raleigh's idea or at least to reduce
the 4s. 0d. to a 2s. 8d. rate for lands under £3 but the official view was

that if 'the meaner taxpayers' were spared no less than two-thirds of the contribution would be lost.

This was the fatal flaw in Elizabeth's fiscal policy, the almost complete failure to tap the increasing wealth of the nation, a failure obscured by the ferocious economies of the queen and Burghley. "Your sovereign," she declared, "is more mindful of your conservation than of herself," or, in other words, she was prepared to put political goodwill before fiscal efficiency. In addition the lengthy and elaborate regulations for assessment and collection showed in practice a declining yield from notoriously inadequate returns. As Sir Walter Mildmay, the Chancellor of the Exchequer, told the House in 1575, "How favourable is the taxation of subsidies whereby far less cometh to the royal coffers than by the law is granted, a matter now known to be so usual that it is hard to be reformed." That no reform had come about by the end of the century is clear from Raleigh's remark in 1601 that "our estates that be £30 or £40 in the Queen's books are not the hundredth part of our wealth". This was not surprising since administration was by the very class which had a vested interest in minimising taxation coupled with a long tradition of avoiding it altogether. The complaint of the Privy Council to the Northamptonshire commissioners in the same year dejectedly summarised the position. "For although Her Majesty doth not expect from you that all men shall be taxed at their just and true values either of the lands or goods, nevertheless in all due consideration there ought to be good regard to be had to assess all men in some far better proportion than hath been done heretofore and nearer to their liability and livings." Even the J.P.'s who had a £20 minimum qualification were blandly assessing themselves at £10 or less.

Money was at the root of the basic instability of Tudor policy. It is true that Henry VII contrived to attain solvency early in his reign and to sustain it but at the expense of administrative equity and his own reputation. Henry VIII secured the acceptance of the subsidy as an adjunct to the tenth and fifteenth, a new and relatively honest set of assessments in 1522 and a steadily increasing customs revenue, but the income from the take-over of monasterial land, which might have sealed his financial independence, was dissipated by improvident sales and an extravagant foreign policy. Finally Elizabeth enjoyed a personal income in, say, 1562 sufficient for peacetime, but even with the most rigid retrenchment she could not sustain a war economy on that revenue alone. She, of all the Tudors, with her statecraft, her personal explanation to her people of why she needed to raise taxes and the constant threat from Spain, might either have developed alternative sources of income such as the granting of monopolies, or reformed direct and indirect taxation instead of relying on outmoded assessments and farming of customs. It was all very well for her to say "She maketh a greater account of the good wills and benevolent minds of. her good and loving subjects than she doth of ten subsidies", but even taking into account inflation and the population explosion, the effects of which were not properly understood, it is ironical that the qualified success of Elizabeth's makeshift financial policy was the source of the eventual bankruptcy of the first Stuart régime.

Chapter VI

Taxation in the Century of Revolutions

The seventeenth century proved to be the most dramatic in English history. It began with the change from Gloriana to a royal pedant, from a popular dynasty to one with ever-narrowing support. The climax of the first phase was the execution of Charles I. But the surrounding twenty years, first of civil war and then of republican rule by a unicameral Parliament, constitued a violent break with the ideal of government which had always been the joint and harmonious rule of the monarch and Parliament. This produced the reaction of the Restoration until the patient compromises of Charles II were undone by the fatal incapacity of James II to prevent division and distrust, which in turn led to the second revolution of 1688. It is a curious paradox that the real successor to the Elizabethan fusion of the power of Crown and Parliament was the enthronement of George I, sealing the triumph of parliamentary supremacy: it is equally paradoxical that, by that time, England had been raised to greatness by the exertions of three very different characters, the regicide, Cromwell, the Dutchman, William and the traitor, Marlborough.

The accession of James I was a critical turning-point in English political history, furnishing as it did an alien dynasty and a new insistence on the divine right of kings. Both innovations could not have come at a more inopportune time when the Commons were beginning to chafe under their role of junior partners in the direction of policy, reinforced by James's record of almost unrelieved failure as a statesman. But in fiscal development the break appears nothing like

82

as decisive: rather the problems which had plagued Elizabeth's last years were intensified under a king who relied on constitutional rights rather than political wisdom.

For example, in periods of financial pressure, James I, as Elizabeth before him, gained relief from land sales and during his reign is estimated to have sold lands worth over £27,000 annually for nearly £650,000. But this policy of parting with capital was not as disastrous as it might have been since there were new acquisitions and increased rentals, although in some cases the old rents persisted until after 1641. Then again the policy of selling isolated or burdensome pockets of land was continued which might decrease revenue marginally but led to marked diminution in administrative costs. Finally, much land was sold with the reservation to the Crown of a rent-charge equivalent to the former yield. The main difference in Tudor and Stuart policy here was a more constant reliance on sales and an increase in transfers so that the net receipts excluding capital sales showed an increasingly substantial fall.

Then again, an auspicious start as far as indirect taxation was concerned, James I's first Parliament made the now traditional grant of the customs subsidies for life. These were currently nearly all under Crown management and formed a major part of the royal revenue, some £127,000 in 1604. As in the previous reign the old desire for 'certainty of revenue' which had haunted Burghley had again begun to possess the Council, and before long there was granted an avalanche of minor leases.

It was imperative, however, to arrive at some decision for the main body of customs. The sixteenth century distinction between London and the outposts had not proved a success: and the logical culmination of the progressive reforms in Elizabeth's reign was the so-called great farm of the customs. This was followed, after consultation with the city merchants, by a revision of the Book of Rates estimated to yield a further £70,000. It was renewed in 1611 at a rent of £136,226, and again for seven years to 1621 in 1614 at an increased rental of £141,000. The final residue of the lease was for five years at £150,000. So far then, both in lands and customs policy, there was a definite carry-over from the Tudor period.

The pattern of direct taxation after 1603 also remained ostensibly the same but significant changes inherent in its basic weaknesses inevitably began to emerge. In the first there was a sharp decrease in the annual collections of the subsidies and the tenths and fifteenths, yielding some £40,000 less than the Elizazethan average. This goes far to explain why Parliament was not summoned to make grants between 1610 and 1621: and although the two subsidies of 1621 brought in £145,000 and the three subsidies and the three tenths and fifteenths in 1624 £278,000, the value of the subsidy had now fallen catastrophically to half its value in Elizabeth's time, quite apart from the drop in real money values. This was partly due to the continued and increasing leniency of the subsidy officials and the practice of making minimum assessments in terms of 20 shillings on land instead of £5 on goods which yielded almost twice the tax. Secondly, James did not understand the ambivalent nature of direct taxation. The traditional parliamentary grant was one subsidy plus two tenths and fifteenths: but in fact Elizabeth had never collected such a levy annually for more than three successive years even in 1601 when Parliament had provided for payment of four grants in four years. James seemed to regard an annual grant as automatic: parliamentary resentment and the disappointing yield forced him into those shifts and expedients characteristic of Stuart fiscal policy.

For the precariousness of royal resources was exposed early in the reign by the controversies over the feudal relics of purveyance, the king's right to purchase 'necessaries' at preferential prices, and wardship, burdens particularly onerous on land-owners. The Commons offered the king an annual sum of £50,000 for relinquishing these legal rights whose practical justification had long vanished: but James, to whom they represented an income of nearly double that sum, was naturally reluctant to agree. The Commons were forced to define their position by their famous Apologia which, apart from its essential constitutional significance, also made specific reference to the grievances arising from antique feudal dues. The Apologia was never published and James's knowledge of it was discreetly veiled in his earnest hope that the House would 'in their own time be careful to see our state supplied by such means as may be most convenient for our weal and the least harmful to our subjects'.

This initial skirmish passed without any overt claim for the power of the purse by Parliament. The next trial of strength came over impositions in Bate's case. The royal powers over the regulation of trade were one way in which James could share the growing wealth of the nation; and Salisbury had cleared debts of £700,000 in this way. Admittedly Baron Fleming and his co-judges had held that no new duties could be imposed for revenue purposes without parliamentary consent: on the other hand, the king could impose regulating duties on foreign imports in the interest of national commerce. This was a fine but sufficient distinction against which merchants like Bate and Chambers appealed in vain.

James, however, was less successful with obtaining revenue from the grant of monopolies which by their nature were far more profitable to the monopolists themselves. They provoked wide and fierce resentment and their proceedings came in for severe censure. Elizabeth had been forced to withdraw her grants and in 1624 James consented to a statute prohibiting the sale of a monopoly in any commodity except new inventions.

Unlike the Elizabethan era when fiscal troubles came to a head at its close, the climax in James's reign was reached in 1610. By then revenue was running short of requirements by some £50,000 annually. Certainly James was extravagant: but if, as the Commons urged, monopolies, purveyance, wardship and other abuses were to be abolished, the revenue from them would have to be replaced.

Neither side would face the realities of the situation. James's initial bid was for compensation of £200,000, basically a reasonable figure but he presented it badly and to the Commons it seemed inordinate: they offered a mere £100,000 plus a debate on impositions which James did not relish. Finally Salisbury coaxed an acceptance of the £200,000 but the whole issue was compromised by the king stepping-up his demands to include liquidation of his debts and a further augmentation of his income besides the jealous preservation of his prerogative. Even this might have proved acceptable if any agreement could have been reached on feasible alternative sources of revenue. The country at large suspected the imposition of a new tax on land, or what were darkly referred to as 'continental taxes'; the French salt tax, for instance, exceeded James's total income: this, in Bacon's phrase, left the Englishman 'least bitten in purse of any nation in Europe'. The attempt, however, at a 'great contract' to compass the fundamental reorganisation of the Stuart financial system, dissolved with Parliament in an atmosphere of mutual mistrust. Yet it must be emphasised that, only a decade or so later, in the last three years of his reign, James, reluctantly forced to embrace the Protestant war policy, reached a height of popularity such as he had not attained since his accession and at his death was probably more popular than Elizabeth in her last years.

Popularity was one thing: but it had completely failed to ameliorate the chronic inadequacy of the royal renenues which was quite another. This was the continuing position on the accession of Charles I. It is impossible to trace the complex fiscal history of the reign through the conventional subdivisions of direct and indirect

taxation: the only intelligible method is to follow and analyse chrono-
logically the desperate shifts and expedients of the king and his
advisers as Parliament sought to cut off each attempt at fiscal escape
until its increasingly grudging and conditional aid was deliberately
set aside.

Initially Charles had every expectation that Parliament would
be ready and indeed anxious to underwrite the war for the Palatinate,
especially as it had assumed the guise of a Protestant crusade, and
since Charles had proved his own good faith by expending the
£278,000 subsidy of 1624, selling lands for £216,000, with a consequent fall in rents, and even disbursing his young queen's £120,000
dowry. He summoned his Parliament of 1625, therefore, confident
that his plea for the sinews of war would have the blessing of a
Parliament which whole-heartedly supported the cause. But
Parliament's strategic ideas differed radically from those of the king.
He was thinking in terms of an expeditionary force: Parliament was
living in an Elizabethan past of piratical expeditions and profits from
privateering. Hence, to Charles's chagrin, they broke with tradition
by granting tunnage and poundage for a year only and a meagre two
subsidies of direct taxation. Charles was forced to expatiate on the
political and economic position: in reply Parliament simply put
redress of grievances as their top priority thus ensuring an abrupt
dissolution. Charles then switched to forced loans under privy seals
and to reviving a custom sanctioned by Elizabethan precedent of
laying the burden and levying and maintaining troops on the county.
Both expedients failed: it was evident the king was 'in such straits for
money as is not to be spoken of': and the more percipient and extreme
of Parliamentarians began dimly to foresee the possibility of holding
their royal master to ransom.

The Parliament of 1626 was as short-lived as its predecessor and
equally unco-operative. Charles was in a conciliatory mood when he
summoned it: but it soon became evident that Parliament was more
interested in Buckingham's impeachment than in grants and that,
considering the inadequate yield of direct taxation since 1621, that
source could no further be relied on for abnormal war finance.
Declaring that 'gold could be bought too dear', he dissolved
Parliament: 'not a minute longer' would he continue the session.

Again, as in the previous year, Charles was thrown back on fiscal
improvisation. His first device was the free gift based on the three
tenths and fifteenths which Parliament would have granted. This was
not a success due to administration by the local justices and the
current trade depression. The initial extension of ship-money only

produced poorly-manned craft which were a disgrace to the navy. But, ignoring the usual fanciful projects, with forced loans, more sales of Crown lands and the solid support of the customs, it seems that close on £1 million was finally made available for the war effort: but even with this prodigious effort, by September 1627 the auditor of the Exchequer of Receipt was writing to Buckingham: 'Pardon me, I beseech you, if I humbly desire that you would advisedly consider of the end, and how far his Majesty's revenue of all kinds is now exhausted. We are upon the third year's anticipation beforehand: land, much sold of the principal: credit lost: and at the utmost shift with the commonwealth.'

Both the political and the financial situations were exacerbated by the military disasters and by the spring of 1628 national bank-ruptcy was perilously close. There was no option but to summon Parliament. Its attitude was instantly predictable. The debates turned on how to prevent the extra-parliamentary levies such as forced loans and aribtrary taxation, and culminated in the Petition of Right when Charles assented to the propostion that 'no man hereafter should be compelled to make any gift, loan, benevolence or suchlike charge without common consent by Act of Parliament'. In return for this major concession, Charles was voted the paltry reward, in the circumstances, of five subsidies, some £275,000. The position then was, after three Parliaments, that in spite of the Petition of Right being an essentially moderate document, each session found the Commons asserting its power a little more, the king, by the same token, being forced on the defensive.

After the dissolution of Parliament in the Spring of 1629 there was little choice before Charles. Finance was still the basic problem. From bitter experience it was clear that the recall of Parliament promised neither fiscal ease nor political comfort. His experiment in dispensing with that body, which was to last eleven years, arose from the failure of direct taxation, the conclusion of peace with France and Spain and the appointment of a new Treasurer, Richard Weston. He had taken up office in 1625 and by 1629 the outlines of his policy were beginning to emerge. Although his term ended in 1635 with his disgrace and death as his venality came increasingly to light, he was a master of expediency, and his reorganisation of the royal finances was based on economy, retrenchment and increase of revenue.

Charles and his advisers had taken a calculated risk in jetti-soning Parliament and its subsidies. From a constitutional point of view no immediate difficulty arose: apart from an aggressive coterie in the Commons there was no organised objection in principle to the king being so economical that parliamentary supplies were not needed. From a fiscal point of view, however, it was essential to compensate for the deficiency in the revenue by means of traditional sources of revenue reinforced by demands for new levies on plea of emergencies. The methods adopted fell into two main categories: those which revived old claims of Common Law and Statute and those which relied on prerogative extension of the law.

The antiquarian revivals included such exactions as the energetic enforcement of distraint of knighthood which netted some £165,000 in the five years from 1630–1635, the restoration of the forest laws the boundaries of which had been subject to gradual encroachment, statutes against enclosures and increased activity in the Court of Wards. Besides these measures, consideration was also given to such bizarre suggestions as the pawning of the Crown Jewels or the levying of an income tax of 2 per cent on incomes over £125. Nevertheless these various procedures should not be overemphasised: they may lend a specious colour to the description of this period of personal rule as the eleven years' tyranny, but, in fact, though they aggravated important persons and classes they were not more than occasional expedients compared with an attempt to secure a permanent and independent income by means of the theories of absolutism.

There were four types of taxation by extension of prerogative which aroused almost the whole nation: of these, benevolences and forced loans, the most violent, had received their death warrant in the Petition of Right. The technique of impositions was inherited by Charles from his father, and he even added to the Book of Rates. The merchants, after a brief interlude of self-denying non-importation, reluctantly admitted the king to a share of their profits at first but later more freely as trade increased. It was only the system of farming taxes which prevented the customs becoming even more lucrative.

The king was less successful in deriving revenue from the sale of monopolies to corporations since he extended the practice to staple articles and outraged not only the merchants but the main body of consumers by these 'plagues of Egypt'. Hence the first concession he had to make in April 1629 was the revocation of commissions, patents and monopolies 'of his mere grace and favour to all his loving subjects'.

Ship-money, however, was the exaction which best represents the period of non-parliamentary rule: it was the most notorious, the most productive and proved the most menacing since screened by law. No wonder it became known as 'the king's great business'. Its perversion of the old duty of maritime defence to an annual cash payment, peculiarly the work of the attorney-general William Noy, almost subverted the Petition of Right and the need to summon Parliament. In 1634 ship-money yielded £104,000: in 1635 and 1636 £200,000. But its very success, legally and economically, dissipated the fiscal lethargy of the community and guaranteed the urgency of opposition. The resistance of Hampden stimulated an increasing reluctance of the public to pay and of the collectors to enforce payment. Once the law, their last guardian, had turned against them, subjects could only abandon legal protest for political action.

Despite the decline in ship-money receipts, the finances, which had begun to overtake arrears in 1635, even showed a small surplus, for the first time in 1636. Even the royal debts had been stabilised by ingenious holding operations. Indeed it is possible that Charles might have enjoyed an indefinite series of balanced budgets, given peace and no abnormal expenditure. His average annual income during the period was some £650,000 which was adequate if no more and which the nation could well afford in the fat years of peace between 1630 and 1640.

What then was the reason for the collapse of prerogative despotism? Certainly Charles's fiscal policy aroused objections; but, apart from the resistance to ship-money, this was mainly passive. Far more significant was the opposition to the Stuart policy of paternal socialism from the growing ranks of capitalists. The basic cause, however, was financial, the ultimate crippling cost of the abortive attempt to impose Anglicanism on the Calvinist Scots, which tilted Charles's precarious balance of receipts and payments decisively against him.

Expenditure on the war itself proved no immediate problem. The years 1639 and 1640 witnessed, the climax of productivity in the Stuart fiscal system, at an estimated £1 million each year. Charles and Juxon, his Treasurer, who doubled the role with Bishop of London, had been careful to see that there were sufficient funds to subsidise a campaign confidently forecast to be short. The real financial crisis came after the failure to achieve military success: and the shrewd Scottish demand for a cash indemnity was the final blow, leaving Charles with no option but to make what terms he could with an angry nation.

The rest is a matter of political and still controversial history. Briefly, when Anglican bigotry caused the collapse of royal power in Scotland, Strafford proceeded to provoke the immediate catastrophe by his fatal delusion that Parliament could still be used as a tool of monarchy. Pym proved his tactical master and engineered the dissolution of the Short Parliament. Before long its three hundred members, reinforced by new Puritan and constitutionist members, came to Westminster with a mandate no previous Parliament had ever possessed. The fiscal measures included a grant of tunnage and poundage accompanied by a declaration that the previous exaction of these duties and impositions had been illegal and must now be levied only with parliamentary consent. Writs of ship-money were likewise illegal: the boundaries of forests were laid down as those prevailing in the twentieth year of James I.'s reign: and finally distraint of knighthood was abolished.

Civil war was still far away, for the king had as yet no substantial following: but as soon as the Long Parliament abolished constitutional abuses, say by August 1641, the fundamental political and religious rifts, which had been papered over in the opposition since the beginning of the struggle against absolutism, began to show. The tradition of nobles such as Digby, the devotion to the law displayed by Hyde, the culture and reverence of land-owners like Falkland, proved incompatible with the Puritan and radical wing which regarded the reforms so far achieved only as a preliminary to revolutionary reconstruction. Thus when Charles declared his allegiance to the Church of England and his resolution 'by the grace of God to die in the maintenance of it' he was spearheading a crusade which won half the country to his side and which sealed his own death-warrant at the same time. Unquestionably economic and fiscal grievances played their part in the origins of the Civil War: but it was the religious factor in the end which created Charles the Martyr.

The outbreak of the Civil War caused an inevitable dislocation in the operation of the royal Exchequer, but there was little change in personnel and no dramatic break in continuity. London was solid for Parliament, and there control of collection continued to be housed: moreover in the last days of Charles this collection had tended to be concentrated in the hands of a few financiers which made it all the easier for the parliamentary commissioners to take over, after exacting a fine of £150,000 for making loans to the king.

God is said to be on the side of the big battalions: the same is true for the side with the longest purse: and this, in the end, was why Cromwell and his army emerged victorious. For although Charles was not desperately short of money in 1642–1643, his private wealth, the gifts of opulent supporters and the forced contributions from country districts all had a desperate once-for-all element and were doomed to rapid exhaustion. In addition many of the Royalist troops were used as tax-gatherers, with disastrous consequences for their discipline and popularity.

Parliament had the simpler task of reorganising the fiscal machine. Its first step was simply to appropriate or raise loans pledging the 'public faith' of the country for their repayment at 5 per cent. There were both compulsory and voluntary subsidy assessments at rates of one-twentieth for real and one-fifth for personal property. A further source of revenue was the fining of vanquished Royalists on one-tenth up to one-third of their estates.

So far the ordinary taxpayer would simply have noted glumly that the change of regime had brought no change in fiscal burdens. In fact two new taxes were instituted which developed considerably under the Protectorate, excise and the Monthly Assessments. In addition, radical changes were made in administration: to look after both the new receipts and the spoils of the Royalist defeat there were ten separate funds charged with both receipts and payments, coordinated by a committee which came to be known as the Treasury Commissioners. This multiplicity of Treasury departments set up by the Long Parliament makes it impossible to construct annual profit and loss accounts during the Civil War. But clearly with London as the greatest source of ready money, command of the sea and thus of the customs at all the ports and the reorganisation of the financial system which by 1644 was yielding regular and substantial revenue, Parliament would never suffer from what Clarendon called 'the incurable disease, want of money' which fatally undermined the Royalist cause.

The fall of Charles Stuart's head, 'with the crown upon it', settled nothing apart from the calling to an account of 'that man of blood' of the Roundheads or the martyr king of the Cavaliers. It alienated at once the law-abiding and traditional beliefs of a civilian nation: and, in the long run, it made the Restoration inevitable since the regicides could never appeal in free election to the people in whose name they had in fact committed an act of revolutionary violence. So with the death of one monarch, another and greater arose as the shadow of Hobbes' Leviathan began to spread over the land.

Certainly the execution made no difference whatever to the basic financial situation except to the extent that the drain of actual warfare had ceased. However, there was still the maintenance of a standing army and the natural inclination of the tax-paying public to assume that the end of campaigning also implied a fiscal armistice. In addition, four years of negotiation and intrigue had ruined the internal unity of the victors which had thrived only on opposition. In the end the Rump of the Long Parliament made the fatal mistake of defying the sovereign army on the vital question of religious reform; and its expulsion left no authority in the land but that of their Captain-General.

Thus there was no immediate financial crisis when Cromwell became Protector. It has been reckoned that Parliament had available from various sources some £6 millions in 1655, ample to fill the gap between an estimated revenue of £2 millions and a maximum annual expenditure of £3 millions. But the Dutch war which had begun in 1652 accelerated the run on reserves: for example the navy alone cost close on £2.5 millions in the three years from 1652 to 1654. Cromwell was no financier: but even if he had been, without the support of Parliament, financial problems, already difficult, were likely to become intractable: as he stated in his speech of 17 September 1656: 'When the Long Parliament ceased to sit, this nation owed £700,000. We examined it: it was brought unto that . . . I believe there was rather more than less.'

Cromwell could count on three principal sources of revenue, of which the first was the faithful standby of customs. Its basic organisation did not need to be elaborate since three-quarters of the dues were levied at the port of London under the supervision of six commissioners who were paid a commission of four-pence in the pound together with interest on advances. They in turn were subject to a Committee for the Preservation of the Customs. Cromwell streamlined this somewhat cumberous structure and included an annual audit and an auditor-general who in 1655 successfully prosecuted one of the commissioners, a Colonel Harvey, who was sent to the Tower for embezzling £30,000.

Receipts remained unsatisfactory, however, with the result that the practice of farming was again suggested: and in the 1658 Parliament a clause was added to the Tunnage and Poundage Bill to give this statutory authority. The opposition argued 'You will destroy the revenue by it and discontent the parties who pay it' but supporters mentioned that 'never were the customs so well paid, nor with so much quiet as when they were let out to farm.' In the event customs remained in the commissioners' hands until the Restoration but the offers by prospective farmers testify to the potential yield. This is generally taken to be in 1653, £350,000, and £400,000 from 1654 onwards. It might be noted that the yield from import duties was about four times that from export duties: and the overall yield reflects the immense expansion of trade. But it was a wasteful system and the differences, averaging £50,000 between the charges and receipts of the customs commissioners and the amounts paid over to the Exchequer, are ample evidence of chronic maladministration.

The two other sources of revenue were both originated by Pym who combined the ability to manage Parliament with fiscal brilliance. Of these the most readily intelligible was the Monthly Assessment, a direct tax of mixed parentage, since it combined features of the old subsidy, the forced loan and the recent ship-money. Originally imposed in 1642 to raise a stated sum weekly, it became monthly in 1645, and by 1649 the amount to be paid by each county had been determined.

The controlling body consisted of local commissioners who decided how to raise the required sum from their district and appointed assessors accordingly: there was also a surveyor, the ancestor of today's Inspector of Taxes. The duty was remitted by the collectors to the Receivers-General which directly funded the military establishment without passing through the Exchequer. Cromwell could thus keep his army firmly under his own command.

The yield of the Monthly Assessments was highly satisfactory, and there seems no doubt that its yield approximated very closely to the assessments made. It was the most successful of all the Cromwellian levies, solving, to a large extent, the problem of how to tax income other than land and banking heavily on willing and unpaid administration by panels of local magnates of whom, until he assumed the Protectorate, Cromwell himself had been a member.

The third source of revenue, and the second brain-child of Pym, was excise, a real innovation as far as this country was concerned although it had existed on the Continent for some time. It had been rejected by the 1628 Parliament, but under the pressure of war the 1643 Parliament passed the first ordinance for levying excise. It was paid by the manufacturer on articles of domestic production and by the first buyer on imports, acting as a sort of customs surcharge. It was immensely unpopular and in 1647 there were 'many tumults and great riots against the receipts and collection of excise.'

After the establishment of the Protectorate six Commissioners for Appeals and Regulating the Excise were appointed. Their duty was principally to supervise the activities of farmers of the tax since by 1659 over half the counties and towns were so administered. The number of dutiable articles also rose until there was little difference between those charged with customs and with excise. There were, however, inevitably frequent changes in rates until the new tax settled down: but even so the net receipts during the Commonwealth exceeded £2 millions.

Ostensibly then Cromwell inherited from the Long Parliament a far more pervasive battery of fiscal duties than his Stuart predecessors had enjoyed, two of which, Excise and the Monthly Assessment, they had never dared to impose: and, while the civil war continued, the citizens, conditioned to regard Commons rather than king as the rightful imposer of taxes, paid these levies with a mechanical indifference.

When Cromwell assumed the Protectorate, however, Parliament reasserted its familiar role of the people's champion against fiscal tyranny, and in 1654 tried to rivet a rigid economy on Cromwell by contriving a budget which purported to show an annual revenue of some £1.2 millions which was judged ample, blandly ignoring counter-calculations showing an actual deficiency of £400,000 annually especially as Parliament's figures envisaged the abolition of the Monthly Assessment. Cromwell promptly dissolved Parliament conceding, however, a further cut in its quota. He had no more success with the 1656 Parliament: and its dissolution in February 1658 was no solution: it was about to be recalled when Cromwell died, leaving his son Richard with a barren inheritance and the immediate, invidious task of finding £20,000 for the Protector's funeral.

Cromwell could not, then, deploy his taxes free of parliamentary consent: he suffered also from their faulty administration. The old controversy of whether or not to farm the indirect taxes was never squarely faced so that customs revenue failed to reach its potential and excise, a new and unpopular tax, had to maintained at comaparatively low rates to justify its description as 'an easy and indifferent levy'. The Monthly Assessment, although efficient, was bound to decline, like the tenth and fifteenth, and the subsidy before it, as the quota was eroded by local changes and national inflation.

Yet these taxes, whatever their theoretical and practical imperfections, marked the end of the financial order of the past three centuries. The sectionalisation of revenue and expenditure whereby the royal demesne provided the normal running costs of the state, customs 'the keeping of the sea' and direct taxation, the abnormal demands of war had been gradually disappearing. While it was still possible to speak of James I 'living of his own', in his son's reign this fiscal cliché lost its validity. Customs had never been allocated solely to the navy: this was simply one of its objects and indeed it was used for political ends by Cromwell to discriminate against France and Spain. Excise was introduced partly and implicitly as a substitute for the feudal dues of the Crown. Finally the Monthly Assessment, although not new in concept or administration, made a major contribution to the break-up of mediaeval finance. Not only was it not subject to Exchequer control but any balance remaining after military disbursement went into a general pool; that is the tax was never sectionalised from its inception. Secondly, despite parliamentary objections, although it was sufficiently like previous direct levies not to attract the hostility of fiscal pamphleteers who concentrated on the innovation of excise and heightened customs dues, it foreshadowed the land tax of the eighteenth century and the income tax of the nineteenth. Thus the Restoration begins with many of the elements of a modern fiscal system and the fiscal moral that to rule without Parliament is to rule without money.

Charles II was brought up sharply against this problem as soon as post-coronation euphoria waned. The short-term difficulty was the deficit of some £3 millions from the Commonwealth of which nearly £1.4 millions related to the forces. There was a hasty grant of a Monthly Assessment of £70,000 for eleven months and a poll tax, estimated to produce £210,000: the bulk of this revenue was assigned to paying off the army and navy as soon as the collectors garnered adequate contributions.

These ad hoc measures, however, were irrelevant to the long-term question of how the king and his government were to be financed. A Commons committee was set up to formulate proposals but its surviving minutes display a remarkable mixture of hard fiscal facts and the most wildly optimistic estimates of what Charles could expect from his loyal subjects. For instance, customs and excise were put at £400,000 and £250,000, heights they were not to achieve for another fifteen years: even had they been accurate, these two major levies, together with miscellaneous sources often more picturesque than profitable, such as a payment from the Society of Music for the right to play before the king left an alarming deficit against an admitted annual expenditure of £1.2 millions on merely peace–time administration. In addition the Crown had now finally accepted the abolition of the Court of Wards apart from "natural fools", and its fees in return for half the excise being settled on Charles for his lifetime and half on the Crown in perpetuity.

As in so much else, Charles II's reign stands between two worlds: the old scale of values in science, philosophy and politics was being challenged by such men as Newton, Locke and Hobbes. This evolution in every department of life was both enriched and complicated by the commanding presence and enigmatic personality of the king. Fiscal ideas were no exceptions: they, too, were undergoing dramatic revisions and the period mirrors both the past and the future. The sources of royal revenue may thus roughly be classified as traditional, experimental or staple.

The 'king's own', not strictly taxation, had almost disappeared apart from the revenues from Lancashire and Cornwall: and the royal fee farm rents, made up of innumerable small items, were sold for £50,000. There was a half-hearted revival of the power to seize two-thirds of recusants' estates in 1674, but little or nothing was effectively done. Nor was the 'free and voluntary' grant of 1661 again resorted to in the reign: the proceeds in any case only amounted to £26,500. Even the old subsidy was resurrected in 1663, for the last time, but inevitably, lacking impartial assessment, the yield was disappointing. Such items, along with taxes on the profits of the post office, on wines, on proceeding at law and on new buildings about London, clearly could not begin to support the cost of running a modern government.

Hence it was not surprising that there should be fiscal experiments. An interesting example was the so-called 'subsidy' of 1670–1671 which was intended to tax income and profits rather than capital and which included a tax on bank deposits: this levy was a failure: its estimated yield was £800,000 but it produced little more than a quarter of that. More profitable were the poll taxes of 1660, 1666 and 1677–1678 which taxed in effect social position, professional status, real and personal property and even the humble hackney coach: here again was the combination of income tax and the expenditure taxes of the succeeding century. Finally there was the ill-fated hearth tax of 1662, a tax of 2s. 0d. annually on each fire-hearth or stove except in houses of an annual value less than £1. Difficulties in collection caused marked fluctuations in receipts, from a mere £34,000 in its first year to almost £200,000 five years later when it was farmed: from then on it averaged some £170,000. It was also subject to evasion and mismanagement: so much so that as early as 1666 the Commons offered to compound for it at eight years purchase on an estimated annual yield of £200,000: and two years later all the farmers of the tax were arrested except one. The harshness of its incidence and abuses in collection forced its abolition immediately after the Revolution of 1688.

Fortunately the staples of customs and excise were gradually strengthening the position of the Crown as the reign progressed. The optimistic estimates of the former reached only £300,000 with some falling off in the two Dutch Wars. From 1674 onwards there was a steady increase up to £500,000 and later some £600,000 annually.

Excise showed a similar trend from £250,000 at the outset of the reign to £400,000 after 1674. Increase in both trade and efficiency of administration explain these rapid rises, but there was constant trouble with farming despite the virtue of the system for obtaining advances of ready money. The importance of Mr. Treasurer Danby here was in remedying the worst abuses of the system and gaining greater control.

Even so, Charles was forced into unorthodox financial manoeuvres. The most notorious was the 'Secret' Treaty of Dover in 1670, making him a pensioner of Louis XIV although he was paid grudgingly and in arrear. Shortage of advances from his tax farmers also explained the 'stop of the Exchequer', two years later, the temporary suspension of repaying loans from wealthy and unpopular merchant bankers and the scaling-down of interest rates.

Although in the last years of his reign, after the dissolution of Parliament in 1681, Charles was solvent, even with French gold he could never have maintained a standing army, the indispensable instrument of tyranny, assuming he had the will to it: he preferred to use his statecraft to provide political ease rather than aggressive absolutism. But James II, despite inheriting an even stronger position fiscally as indirect taxation continued to increase, could only improvise a despotism which fell at the concerted rallying-cry of 'No Popery'.

The seventeenth century was a period of fiscal as well as political revolution. When it began the king had his proprietory and feudal revenues, an antique stereotyped system of direct taxation still regarded as extraordinary, and customs duty on goods. By 1688 the 'king's own' had virtually disappeared, the Monthly Assessment and allied taxes were foreshadowing more realistic versions of direct taxation and Customs, in the indirect field, had been powerfully reinforced by Excise. These profound changes did not mean that the chronic inadequacy of revenues had now been solved: the immediate effect of the flight of James II was that no longer could the monarch stamp his personality on fiscal policy which had literally been his prerogative for the past four centuries. The long-term result of fiscal changes, in the shift of emphasis to indirect taxation, was to break the long tradition of exempting the poor which had grown up during the Tudor and Stuart periods, and which an unpopular Excise was now eroding.

But the argument that a man's total expenditure is an equitable test of his taxability was supported by theorists such as Hobbes and Sir William Petty long before the Meade Report. The latter was certainly the most important writer on taxation before Adam Smith and his influence extended well into the eighteenth century. The 'Glorious Revolution', in fiscal terms, buried prerogative as an inexhaustible treasury of arbitrary taxation: it also, reinforced by current fiscal thought, tended to favour a taxation system which spared the land, but, by the same token, not the poor.

Chapter VII

Fiscal Paternalism

The years from 1689 to 1798 were more stable and more sober than the previous two centuries. The 1688 Revolution provided only a makeshift settlement since the Bill of Rights was basically an assertion of traditional liberties; and even by 1714 finality seemed as far away as ever. But by 1727, with the untroubled accession of the second Hanoverian and the continuance of Walpole's soothing régime, the furious brilliance which had given England the reputation of the most capricious nation in Europe faded into the cold dawn of accepted compromise. The dualism of loyalties and the merciless party struggles of landed and mercantile interests abated into more civilised encounters in the Commons for the monopoly and perquisites of political power. As the century moved on, in forty-five years of war England doubled her Empire, lost most of it, then began to acquire a second greater than the first. The supremacy of Parliament was consolidated by the fiscal and military exigences of government, while the National Debt and the Bank of England underpinned the change in the structure of capital and finance which made possible the industrial revolution.

Indirect taxation remained the mainstay of the revenue and, of the two major levies, customs was by far the older although slightly the less profitable. Quite apart from revenue-raising, it was being used increasingly to discourage imports of commodities which could be produced at home or which were incapable of further processing here: in addition it acted as a luxury tax. Generally speaking its rate was five per cent on a miscellaneous collection of imports and exports although, to promote home industry, export duties were gradually abolished.

When farming ceased in 1671 the Customs Board had been reconstituted with seven Commissioners at salaries of £2,000 and other high officials including a Solicitor and a Secretary. The Bristol Collector was the highest paid of his colleagues at £400: others had annual remuneration of something less than £200, but the majority of the staff rarely topped £50. The establishment itself was split into Headquarters housed in Wren's new Custom House, the London Pool and the Outports staff: this last would normally consist of a collector, a comptroller, a land and tide surveyor plus tidesmen and boatmen with occasionally a smack attached to the port manned by a captain, six men and a boy. Riding officers were a later addition giving the service increased mobility.

The piecemeal succession of Acts and regulations were to an extent regularised at the beginning of the period when there was an all-round increase of rates by means of subsidies which effectively doubled them, together with special taxes on specific objects. Staff, however, remained at the same level which gave still further opportunities for smuggling. This activity was partly conditioned by high tariffs, but even more by the profitability of obtaining goods not legally importable such as French wines and textiles during the war with Louis XIV, for example. So rife did smuggling become that one of the reasons for Walpole's Excise Bill was to enlist the aid of the Excise men for the hard-pressed Customs officers, who were already calling in the army to support them.

Smuggling was no more easy to check on the high seas or coastal waters for the preventive ships, which had to be out in all weathers, were usually of heavy burden and could be outsailed by the lighter smuggling vessels. Walpole's new book of rates made illegal activities more profitable and although the reward for seizures was half the proceeds for sale which encouraged the private venturers, the smugglers simply equipped themselves with larger ships: and Customs found they were involved in a miniature armaments race with their resolute opponents.

For the government could not afford any decrease in customs revenue which was generally accepted as being the most convenient form of levy. As Pelham put it when proposing on 8 February 1748 'a new impost of poundage upon all goods imported' the duty was easily paid, since merchant importers were 'all men of considerable fortunes and extensive credit'; it was therefore possible to make a reasonable estimate of the yield and it would 'in no way affect the poorer sort of our people'. It is interesting to note that, later on in the debate, Fox agreed that the increase was the most prudent fiscal course as 'no minister will dare increasing either the land tax, the window tax or the number of our excises'.

In the succeeding years, however, under pressure of war, customs increased in complexity as its yield was stepped-up, until in 1784 Pitt initiated a wholesale attack on smuggling together with a scientific rearrangement of the tariff: he followed this up three years later, in his 1787 Budget, with the Bill for the Consolidation of Customs and Excise which revised the whole of the tariff which involved no less than 3,000 dutiable articles. In the process of reform the fundamental basis of customs was changed: instead of the value of items imported, tax was now levied on each specific item. Goods could now be bonded and duty paid not at the time of importation but when the merchant found less onerous. In all, simplicity in incidence, efficiency and economy in collection characterised the new rate-book which was to prove its value in the long struggle with France between 1793 and 1815. At the outset of the period Customs raised some £640,000: a short decline during the first French war (1690–1697) was followed by a steady rise from 1697 and by 1713 the yield was £1.5 millions: it rose to more than double that sum by the close of the period.

The second major indirect levy was excise which had never been popular: and dislike of it grew after 1683 when it ceased to be farmed mainly because the state Excise men were both more efficient and more ruthless. The duty was levied internally mainly on such necessaries as malt (for brewing), candles, leather, salt and soap. The advantages of excise were two-fold: since food was cheap, the increase in duty did not impose an intolerable rise in the cost of living and the levy itself was not saddled with any traditional commitments. It was therefore rapidly increased and extended in scope after 1688 and made a major contribution towards war finances: but by the end of Anne's reign there was a certain downturn in receipts indicating that possibly the limit of taxation had been reached. However, by administrative improvements, in particular the setting up in 1723 of bonded warehouses for tea, coffee and cocoa, the yield began to rise appreciably.

It was the success of these warehouses which led to one of the most significant incidents in the history of excise during the period when Walpole proposed, ten years later, in his Excise Bill, to extend the practice to wines and tobacco. His motives were simply to increase revenue, to check evasion and smuggling, and perhaps to pave the way for the gradual abolition of land tax. The storm of protest raised, skilfully fomented by the Opposition, was out of all proportion to the potential demands of the suggestion. In the end Walpole dropped the Bill with the comment that 'the thing was lost by not being generally understood: and interested men, supported by angry men, prevailed by raising false alarms'. In fact he went further and defended his policy in a pamphlet, where, basing his Apologia on the thesis that 'the best taxes are those that are the easiest borne', he argued that the proposals were the only way to stop the 'notorious, monstrous and abominable frauds', which left nearly two-thirds of the items which should have borne tax in practice unduted. The episode is generally written off as a powerful minister being coerced by clamour and opinion: but, fiscally speaking, it postponed the possibility of a general reform for fifty years.

Walpole, however, might hardly have been the man to undertake it, judging by another illuminating conflict during the seventeen thirties over the re-imposition of the salt tax. This had been repealed in 1730 'giving ease,' as George II had declared in the King's Speech, 'where the duties are most grievous', but was restored two years later as part of a two-pronged attempt to reduce or even get rid of land tax of which the ill-fated Excise Bill had been the other half. The ensuing controversy raised all the basic questions in current taxation and was recognised to do so, for Walpole was deliberately altering the existing incidence of fiscal measures. Walpole's defence was that everyone should pay taxation since everyone shared in the protection and the services afforded by the state. He agreed that the burden should be in proportion to 'circumstances and condition in life' although it was not clear how this was to be achieved: he thought, however, that salt tax was 'a more just, a more equal and a better proportioned tax' than land tax which he stigmatised as 'the most unusual, the most grievous and the most oppressive tax that ever was raised in this country'.

The Opposition maintained that Walpole's policy was harmful both to the poor and to trade, but in general the pleas were more emotional than doctrinal: certainly there was no suggestion from either side that the poor should never pay taxes in any circumstances. The argument that the tax would increase wages and thus enhance the cost of manufactured goods carried more weight: but it was not difficult to show that wages had not diminished when the tax was repealed in 1730 and that the argument, although possessing a specious logic, was not economically sound. The real objection to the reintroduction of the salt tax was that if Walpole wanted a further half million in taxation, land tax offered an easy way with no further administrative cost; unlike salt tax which was expensive to run and required the reinstallation of a complex executive mechanism.

After this flurry of activity between 1730 and 1735, the excise duties settled down and there were few significant changes either in rates or dutiable articles until the Napoleonic war period later in the century. Then, as with customs, the old taxes on beer, salt, candles, leather, coal and soap were increased. The yield of excise had always slightly exceeded customs at over £3 millions by the end of the period: and the Bill for the Consolidation of Customs and Excise not only instituted much needed reforms but made possible a national profit and loss account over which Parliament and Treasury could exercise effective control.

In the field of direct taxation during the period, land tax, following the rapid failure of other direct taxes after 1688, was the paramount feature. It had a distinguished, if possibly obscure, ancestry: it was politically and fiscally controversial: other direct levies subsequently tried were very much supplementary: and, most important, its organisation was taken over, at the end of the century, by the newly-fledged income tax. But purely in terms of yield it was comparatively unproductive and its elaborate hierarchy of paid and unpaid officials was both cumbersome and, often enough, ineffective.

Danegeld or possibly scutage may arguably be considered as the 'original' land tax which is itself a convenience title. There was certainly a land tax of sorts during the reign of Richard II which had its expected yield standardised in 1344 under Edward III. It is understandable, then, that fiscal historians faced with a variety and antiquity of choice, should have debated the ostensible sources of land tax. But even the origins of the best-known land tax, that of the eighteenth century, had been wrongly attributed. The initial error by the early historians was dating the land tax from 1692 although there were complaints that its provisions were very unclear and confused: some of the confusion might have been cleared by looking at the Acts at the opening of the reign. The error was repeated and enlarged by the Royal Commission on the Income Tax of 1920 which remarked casually that 'the land tax had been in existence since 1692'. Later fiscal historians were similarly bemused by the 1692 myth, and happily repeated the legend of the 'original' Land Tax Act of that year. The fact is that the so-called 'original' Land Tax Act of 1692 was not so called, it was not original and its taxation was by no means limited to lands. All its charging sections are basically to be found in I Will. & Mar. C20 of 1688. That Act imposed a rate of 1s. 0d.; this was followed by Will. & Mar. Sess.2. C.1 which imposed a rate of 2s. 0d.; finally another Act of the same year /Sess. 2 C5 added a fourth shilling. So 1689 not 1692 was the first year of the revived land tax.

The importance of the Act of 1692 seems to be that the quota of each district was fixed on the returns for that year and remained substantially unchanged for the next century. It is interesting to note finally that details of the amounts raised under the head of land tax date from the accession of William and Mary onwards, that is the 1688 start is taken for granted. Secondly, it is now almost forgotten that its scope included offices, stock, merchandise and specie on a capital value of 6 per cent.: but in practice land was the principal subject of assessment since it could not be concealed. The fact that the tax became popularly titled a land tax was a confession of failure by the state to make personal property and incomes, as opposed to realty, pay their fair share.

Theoretically, however, the aids from the beginning of the reign of William and Mary were designed as general taxes on income. Liability was attached in the first place to income arising from estates in ready money or debts or in goods, wares, or any other personal estate: after deducting 'desperate debts and moneys bona fide owing' the rate was 4s. 0d. in the pound and 24s. 0d. on each £100's worth of goods. The second subject of assessment was offices of profit (except serving officers in the armed forces), also taxable at 4s. 0d. in the pound. Finally, all incomes from land were assessed at the rack-rental value, without any deduction for repairs or other burdens, the tax being paid by the tenant and deducted by him when paying his rent to the landlord. The Act furnished particulars of the amounts required from each county and city. London, of course, rated the highest assessment of £8,583 2s. 8d. Yorkshire rated the highest county at nearly £7,000 with Devon, Essex and Middlesex (including Westminster) not far behind at over £6,000. The town of Haverford West brought up the rear with an allocation of £36 6s. 10d. These assessments were often far from accurate, especially in the more distant counties and the fixed quota finally imposed in 1698 came none too soon as the tax yield had declined considerably in five years.

The central responsibility for the overall supervision of tax collection was vested in the Tax Office and 'Their Majesties' Agents for Bringing in of Taxes', whose duty was, briefly, the 'due and speedy getting in of Taxes': and immediately under their control were the Receivers-General responsible for the tax of a particular county or town, under surety, and for forwarding it to the Exchequer. They also supervised the performance of the Collector and his remissions of tax to his appropriate Receiver-General. The Agents were also concerned to stimulate the local Commissioners, the gentry concerned in the day to day management of the taxes, in the execution of their statutory duties and to advise them on points of law and questions in dispute with the assistance, if necessary, of the Attorney-General.

These Commissioners, under varying titles, had always been an integral part of the machinery of direct taxation in England. They were appointed by name in the Act and were almost entirely the landed notables of the district, although there was an occasional 'Gent.' or 'Dr. of Physick'. They met within a fortnight or so of the Act becoming law, their principal function being to decide what number should act in each division, which was their administrative unit and who should be authorised to report to the Receivers-General 'a schedule of the sums assessed'. Inevitably the Commissioners tended to show partiality, but these administrative defects could often prove a useful safety valve.

The two officials in the field were the Assessor and the Collector, both appointed by the Commissioners. The duties of the former were implicit in his title and Commissioners were enjoined 'that in your respective Divisions will please to take especial care to appoint able, conscientious and knowing persons for the Rates (of tax)'. The Assessor, having made his assessments, had to deliver a copy to his Commissioners who then signed two duplicates, of which one went to the Collector so that the process of getting in the tax could start. The Collector was authorised commission at 3d. in the pound which afforded him every inducement to reach his quota. The Commissioners could permit distress when duty was unpaid and presaging TMA, s.20C empower their Collectors 'to break open any door and any chest, trunk, box or other things': they could even authorise imprisonment except in the case of peers. The Collector was also examined by the Commissioners on his receipts and could be proceeded against when necessary.

An appeal procedure was laid down and, as further protection to the taxpayer, he could claim damages for unjust or vexatious assessments. Minor administrative points were not overlooked: if a man had his house in one parish and his goods in another he was to be assessed where he dwelt. Finally there was even provision for the amount undercollected to be floated as a loan at 7 per cent. The importance of this elaborate mechanism from the Agents to the hunble Collectors was that it provided a ready-made framework for the real income tax a century or so later.

Up to 1715 land tax was gradually winning a grudging accept-ance: there was opposition from the peers in 1693, but no real difficulty with succeeding Bills. Parliament was never reluctant to vote money for war purposes especially when corn price stayed high, unless particular campaigns were going badly. It was a fiscal paradox of this period that a predominantly landed party should be imposing a disproportionate tax on land. From 1715, however, began the long decline in the fortunes of land tax. It could still be an inflammatory issue in principle, but the rates at which it was levied and its low key yield and administration show how little of a real burden it must have been. The full rate of 4s. was levied once only, in 1725, during the period up to 1740, the result of Walpole's stern efforts to reduce or even abolish it. It fell to 2s. in 1755 and subsequently alternated between 3s. and 4s. These fluctuations in rates were not so important as the decline in receipts which slumped to £1.3 millions in 1774, attained a maximum in 1781 at nearly £2 millions and fell back to an average of £1.5 millions in the years before its conversion in 1798 to a perpetual rent-charge at 4s. 0d. with provision for redemption, and in this form the tax lasted on into the 20th century (FA 1963, s.58).

The gradual obsolescence of land tax both as a fiscal weapon and a political counter was paralleled inevitably by an equally gradual falling off in adminisrative efficiency both locally and centrally. The earliest letters from the Agents for the Bringing in of Taxes amply illustrate the vital need to combat delays whether on the part of the Commissioners in delivering their duplicates, of the Collectors in making their payments to the Receivers–General or, as is most common, of the Receiver-General in remitting to the Exchequer. Here is a typical example to a Receiver–General: 'We received yours of the 27th ultimo wherein you take notice of the remiss execution of the Act within the County of Gloucester which we find is not only in your county but all England over'. It is clear that from an early date administrative complaints were justified arising partly from the pursuit of arrears 'not one penny paid", as another letter runs, 'to the great disservice of their Majesties'. It is equally clear that the attempt to tax incomes had little success: civil servants who could not conceal their salaries were permitted by the Treasury to have their tax refunded and charged to office incidents. The tax had always been unpopular with the landed classes; and Walpole's comparative success in keeping the rates low could not be sustained in the period of endemic warfare which followed his regime. Secondly, the central control also began to lose the personal oversight which had guided the tax through its first years: the vigour of the first Agents was missing and their successors lacked their long experience. The manuscript material for this latter period is diminished both in quality and quantity: gone are such pungent comments as 'You either do not remember what letters you write to us or do not read the answers you have been sent otherwise you would not press us so often when we have given you our opinion', for querulous and ineffective complaints which drew from the Treasury the tart criticism that 'their Lordships will be obliged to take vigorous methods for the public money unless they find from their admonishment some good effect'. Reforms were suggested following the Report on Land and Assessed Taxes in 1780 but nothing decisive was done. No tax could maintain its validity with its income provisions flouted, its double taxation sections on non-jurors and Catholics invidious and its direction without any real sanctions. Finally there was the failure of local organisation at all levels. The Commissioners were partial at best and corrupt at worst, using their influence to avoid making their fair contribution to the tax quota: the discontent thus aroused they stifled by holding appeal meetings only infrequently. They also relaxed their watch on their Collectors which meant in turn the efficiency of the Receivers–General was impaired. The stimulus applied by the original Agents had now long departed and the Treasury confessed bitterly that they did not know of an instance of a Receiver of the land tax being dismissed merely for being remiss in his payments or in arrear. Towards the end of the period the Commissioners even began to descend in the social scale, a process highlighted by the "Coventry scandal" of 1798 when a list of the land tax Commissioners was found to contain journeymen, weavers, scavengers, dealers in horseflesh and cats' meat, dealers in dung, paupers on parish relief, two 'fidlers' and two idiots. The fact was that the sustained effort of holding a high rate of collection had proved too much for amateur administration and the limits of the type of direct taxation, created at the time of the Revolution, had been reached.

Of the other direct taxes existing at the time of the Revolution, poll tax was the oldest and the first to disappear. Rates were based on a scale of rank, not income or expenditure, and there were several levies between 1689 and 1698 as an adjunct to the aids. The average yield was about £400,000, although it should have been at least double: the fault was bad administration and partiality by the Commissioners. But it was a backward–looking tax, and, although a revival of it was proposed in 1758 by a Treasury Secretary, it was never levied after 1698.

Land tax was not thus left in sold possession of the direct taxation field, however. In 1696 the window tax was introduced originally to cover losses in the coinage through clipping and wear: it was imposed on "windows or lights" and extra large windows over twelve feet high were charged as two. The rates were modest at first, being 2s. 0d. per house plus 4s. 0d. if it possessed more than ten but less than twenty windows, 8s. 0d. if there were twenty windows or more. It was a crude tax but with a useful potential for expansion and its rates were increased at regular intervals. These increases just about held the yield steady owing to evasion: as the preamble to the Act of 1766 admitted 'the revenue arising hath for some years past greatly decreased and the same is still likely to diminish'. Payment of the tax was quarterly, ironically enough, on feast days. The highest yield was £454,960 in 1782 but the norm was an average between some £400,000 and £435,000.

Apart from evasion, the Reports from the Commissioners of Taxes between 1739 and 1743 show how unsatisfactory the local administration was. There were innumerable appeals on the subject of stopping-up lights which, owing to the partiality of local jurisdiction, had to be referred to the High Court. Dummy windows incidentally were not necessarily stopped-up windows. They were often adopted as a feature in the design of eighteenth century buildings to preserve classical symmetry. General surveyors were sending no account of their surveys although required to do so: and thirty-seven of their surveyors were negligent and incapable: one was 'so taken in another employment that he had no leisure to perform any part of his surveyor's duties and his books are crowded with errors'. Despite the many objections to it, however, it became the mainstay of what came to be known as the Assessed Taxes.

Still under the heading of direct taxation might be mentioned the fiscal curiosity of the Act of 1694 for taxing 'Marriages, Births and Burials . . . and Bachelors and Widowers for the term of five years for carrying on the war against France with vigour'. This Marriage Act, as it came to be known, imposed a sliding scale of liability ranging from peers to commoners: but the basic rates were four shillings on burials, only half the price on births, two shillings and sixpence for marriages while the single man or widower paid only one shilling. It came into force in 1695, in the first place for a period of five years, but was later extended to 1706. Little is known about the actual mechanism of collection. Bachelors and widowers could pay in two instalments: payments for both marriages and deaths would normally be made soon after the qualifying event. As for administration it is interesting to note that the Act adopted the land-tax mechanism of Commissioners, surveyors, assessors and collectors. The scale, of course, was very much smaller but it is one more illustration of how strong was the tradition of co-opting local administration.

The fiscal pattern of the eighteenth century can thus be presented as neatly divided between indirect and direct taxation, the former covering customs and excise and the latter land tax as well as ancillary levies which might be long or short-lived. But such a division is altogether too tidy. It overlooks the significance of the administrative scene, the contemporary financial revolution, the wealth of literature and of conflicting theories on fiscal matters and the frenzy of fiscal improvisation which triggered off the American Revolution and which later was summarised in the Triple Assessment of 1798, the direct ancestor of the income tax of the following year. If the history of taxation in the eighteenth century is too rigidly compartmentalised, it conceals the element of continuity vital to understanding nineteenth century developments.

The nearer what appears to be a comparatively modern taxing apparatus approaches the easier it is to forget that, although the post-Revolution period had seen a certain reorganisation of the Treasury, partly stimulated by William III who attended there thrice monthly and partly to cope with the increased revenue from customs, excise and aids to finance the wars against France, these were the last reforms for nearly a century. The administrative machinery remained a strange mixture of mediaeval techniques and pragmatic innovations. Roman numerals and the Courthand an almost unreadable script, were still formally used at the Exchequer and so too were tallies. Indeed it is maintained that the Treasury did no sort of budgeting thus depriving the government of a major tool of financial policy. Certainly the word 'budget' does not appear to have been used until 1733 and not commonly until 1750, but there was definite ministerial direction from 1691 onwards, obviously not in the form of a comprehensive Budget speech but in 'humble suggestions' to the Treasury from senior civil servants which increased rapidly in volume after 1709. The traffic was not all one way: Godolphin, the First Lord of the Treasury, was writing to the Commissioners of Customs and Excise "to prepare schemes and proposals of the earnest and most plausible ways for raising money for the support of next year's expenses." In fact the Treasury Papers of the period contain estimates of public expenditure, corrected and annotated probably by the Secretary William Lowndes. There was plenty of direction from the Treasury: that it was not always taken was not the fault of its cogency but of party faction.

The Revenue Commissioners and the Tax Office could not show the same degree of professionalism. Not a great deal of research has been done on the Commissioners themselves: The Duke of

Wellington, when a half-pay colonel, fortunately had his application rejected. The majority seem to have been appointed on account of family, local and even occasionally royal interest. But the expert element was never completely lacking: and, through the example of public servants such as Lowndes, the pristine traditions of duty and efficiency began to revive. Running the department, however, was hampered by a perennial shortage of staff. In 1715 there were four Commissioners, a solicitor, a secretary, four clerks, a 'well-paid housekeeper', a deputy and a porter. The complement was the same in 1780 and even by 1797, despite the increase in taxation, the office staff had only risen to fourteen. No wonder when other departments rejoiced in a month's holiday, the Taxes' staff could take none. Fortunately a local representative of the central government was beginning to emerge in the person of the surveyor, a shadowy figure at first, but with important duties under the window tax of 1696 and gradually utilised more and more as taxes began to multiply. The life of a surveyor could be hard. "They suffered", ran a contemporary report, "from accidents in falls from horses on hard roads or lying in damp beds on their survey". But provided they were not allowed too much automomy and their supervising Inspectors exercised proper control over them they reacted well to their new responsibilities and were to become the keystone of Pitt's new financial arch.

Despite inevitable increases in the rates and subject of taxation, these never became as onerous as they might have been owing to the ease and cheapness of borrowing: and although credit facilities were to a certain extent defective and could result in wild speculation, borrowing enabled England to spend far more on war than was consonant with the tax revenue. 31 per cent of the Spanish Succession War was financed by public loan, 37 per cent of the Seven Years War and no less than 40 per cent of the American War of Independence. Fortunately the price level was falling so that inflation was minimal. It was only when the National Debt, to which so much taxation was geared, began to reach alarming proportions that Pitt was forced to consider a more effective addition to direct taxation.

Not that Pitt, or indeed any of his predecessors, had been lacking advice from fiscal economists. As early as 1662 Sir William Petty, the economist, had maintained "It is generally allowed by all that men should contribute to the public charge but according to the share and interest they have in the public peace; that is, according to their estates or riches." But clearly, with the current emphasis on indirect taxation, a man of means who lived below those means avoided his fair share of taxation whereas a poor man could not avoid paying taxation where imposed on necessities. Locke summarised early thinking on the subject when he stated "Everyone who enjoys his share of the protection should pay out of his estate his proportion for the maintenance of it." The fallacy was, of course, that the rich paid proportionately less than the poor relative to respective means. John Cary, another economist, came nearer the truth when he argued that excise made the poor "pay more than the wealthiest of their neighbours, suitable to what they have: for though a rich man spends more in excisable things than a poor man doth, yet it is not his all, whereas the other's poverty gives him leave to lay up nothing."

The eighteenth century inherited a system of taxation based on indirect levies with a tinge of abnormality or emergency still attached to direct taxation as, for example, the invariable preambles to William III's aids "for the purpose of carrying on a vigorous war against France". With such a system the fiscal axiom that all men should pay tax was a natural concomitant: and for the first part of the century Walpole, in his attempt to minimise the direct levy of land tax at the expense of the indirect levy of salt tax, was simply following current fiscal trends. The opposition in Parliament to this policy has already been commented on: and, shortly after the debate, this intrinsically emotional appeal was reinforced by a theory with more commercial attraction, that the necessaries of a poor man's subsistence should be exempted to keep wages low for the benefit of trade. Pamphleteers argued the need for reducing labour rates which depended on the price of food and drink in order to increase the volume of internal and external trade, or the virtue of a single tax on houses with exemption for the poorest people "that thereby their labour might become so much the cheaper, and the goods which are the product of their labour sold at a lower rate than can be afforded by most nations." Unfortunately for this ingenious theory, in practice wages did not rise or fall with tax fluctuations on necessaries; but even so, in a less crude form, this concept lingered on. The combination of compassion for the poor and the assumed economic advantages of exempting necessaries led inevitably to the emergence of what appeared to be an ideal form of taxation, levy on luxuries: and the greater part of tax literature in the period testified to the general acceptance of this doctrine. "Every man's contribution", said Adam Smith, "is altogether voluntary, it being in his power to consume, or not to consume, the commodity taxed." There was, in addition, an attractive moral overtone in such taxation as it acted in a general way as a sumptuary law.

Not all these taxes, which began to proliferate from the sixties on, could be justified either by their success or by eighteenth century fiscal canons, however. By then the need for a financial readjustment in relations between the American colonies and the mother country was apparent, for there was a latent contradiction between the former's ambitions for autonomy and the latter's mercantile code. The stamp duties were simply an attempt to make the colonies pay for their own defence, but as Alistair Cooke puts it, "It was the first internal tax that Britain had ever proposed and its effect was to rouse the colonists to a fury." It was repealed within a year but later repressive laws and import dues made it clear that the government intended to raise revenue in America. Another outburst of fury led to a second withdrawal which provoked the accusation that the taxes had been removed to flood the colonies with cheap goods. This is not the place to recount the story of the American War of Independence, fought with such extraordinary incompetence on both sides: sufficient to say that when it was over, the United States had been born, and the British National Debt had increased by £114 millions.

The advancing century, then, seemed only to bring fresh disasters and increasing disorganisation in the national finances. Customs and Excise, indeed, profited from increasing consumption and their later reorganisation. But direct taxation was static in yield and expansion was only to be looked for, in view of current fiscal thinking, in expenditure taxes. The first of these was the tax on persons keeping carriages of 1747 which was progressively increased during the Napoleonic wars: the tax on the possession of plate, however, of 1756 was a comparative failure and was repealed in 1777. It was in that year, however, that the expenditure taxes began in earnest. In 1777 came the tax on servants, in 1778 the inhabited house duty, 1784 a tax on pleasure horses – and racehorses, the latter consisting of a basic levy on all starters plus an additional levy on winners, 1785 a tax on female servants together with a tax on sporting licences and gamekeepers. Declaration of war in 1783 provoked the tax on hair powder of 1795, the tax on dogs in the following year, the tax on clocks and watches of 1797 which had to be repealed in the following year, having had a disastrous effect on the industry, and was replaced by the tax on armorial bearings. One of the heaviest and most productive taxes was that on spirits, originally imposed for the dual purpose of industrial development and revenue but later for the purpose of lessening consumption. Pitt steadily increased the rates, saying in 1796 "the consumption is so pernicious that with respect to this article no man could wish there should be any limits to the duty, as far as is consistent with the means of safely collecting it."

These desperate fiscal expedients were clearly inadequate as war expenditure intensified and since Pitt was now proposing that the major part of each year's deficit should be funded within the year. The scene was set for a revival of direct taxation which the interests of the commercial classes had managed so far to postpone. For behind the theme of luxury taxation had always persisted the ground-bass of a general direct tax. As soon as the tax on incomes, such as it was, ceased in 1712, some of the fiscal economists broke away from the main stream in favour of a direct general income tax. In 1738 William Wood wrote "An Enquiry" for an income tax and later put forward a proposal "for a true Income Tax with exemptions and abatements and allowances for children". The "Gentlemen's Magazine" of 1763 recommended an equal tax on the general income of the kingdom. Adam Smith himself was not opposed to income tax in theory: indeed it was his first principle that taxation should be distributed in proportion to income: his objection, in which he voiced the opinion of the majority of his fellow-countrymen, was that it involved "an inquisition more intolerable than any tax".

Now, although Pitt had studied the "Wealth of Nations" and had been influenced by Lord Shelburne who had discussed income tax with him as early as 1785, neither he nor any of the eighteenth century advocates of income tax were putting forward something which had originated in the minds of any one of them. The current revival of interest in income tax was due to the dixiéme or tenth of Louis XIV imposed in 1710 on all incomes under four schedules, realty, salaries, securities and businesses. Further, Pitt was not an early or an easy convert, but exhausted every possible resource before abandoning the voluntary principle for compulsion. The bulk of the expenditure taxes were now massed under the generic heading of the Assessed Taxes. The rates of these, the wine and spirit duties, import duties including sugar and tea were all raised between 1795 and 1797. But the real breach in the hallowed principle of voluntaryism came in 1798 and it is essential to understand precisely what the so-called "Triple Assessment" entailed.

Pitt used the 1797 return of an individual's taxable establishment as the basis for the 1798 assessment to prevent possible evasion by making false current returns. In spite of the Triple Assessment's name the number of years' assessments covered by the same basis year was not always three; it could be as high as five. Previously these Assessed Taxes could be regarded as voluntary since by foregoing such luxuries in any one year, tax was avoided in the following year. Now the host of impositions, once payable at will, were suddenly converted by Pitt into compulsory taxes at greatly increased rates. But half a century's voluntaryism could not so easily be discarded since Pitt compromised by providing for exemption or abatement by reference to annual income returnable on a prescribed form. In substance the charge was on the lower of the Triple Assessment or of a proportion of annual income, which was generally one-tenth; for incomes in the £60 to £200 range it was on a sliding scale, with complete exemption below £60. This tempered the effect somewhat: but clearly it was not a very long step from limiting high expenditure taxes to one-tenth of total income to taxing simply one-tenth of total income.

The Triple Assessment was not a success: its yield was only half that expected and it had to be buttressed by patriotic charity. Even at this late hour Pitt was still not converted: "If the amount of every man's property could be ascertained it would be a most desirable thing to make the people contribute to the public exigence in proportion to their wealth. But there existed no means of ascertaining the property of individuals, except such as were of a nature not to be resorted to." By autumn of 1798 he had begun to work on the "Heads of a Plan for a Contribution" based on yield statistics from the Treasury. On December 3, 1798 he introduced his income tax: the Triple Assessment was repealed and the new levy was to be effective from the new year.

Legislation during the eighteenth century was detailed but not complex. Indirect taxation, principally customs and excise, was little changed except under pressure of war: direct taxation was stereotyped in the shape of the land tax until 1798. New taxation was roughly of two types, the expenditure or luxury taxes which fell mainly on the wealthy, and those which affected all classes such as the house and window taxes, the additions to the beer and malt duties and the spirit duty, the rate of which had moral overtones. Opinion in the period was represented by three basic ideas, that all should pay taxes, a hangover from the seventeenth century, that the poor should be exempt on compassionate grounds, and that necessaries should not be taxed for the commercial advantage of keeping wages down. The second and third of these ideas were exemplified in the sumptuary taxes from carriages to plate, which also embodied the vital element of voluntaryism. Such a system could finance a peacetime economy but was totally inadequate for war. Fortunately the idea of a direct income tax had never been wholly lost: and there existed also a fiscal bureaucracy capable of running it with the distilled experience of generations of prosperity and adversity, providing a fixed point of reference behind the kaleidoscope of politics.

Chapter VIII

The Emergence of Income Tax

The late Georgian and the Victorian times, covering almost a century from 1799 to 1895, are the best known and most written about of any period in British history. Perhaps it is because they are so lavishly documented or perhaps because it is now possible to see the age more clearly and dispassionately as historical perspective widens. It is a very minor Victorian figure who cannot boast a clutch of biographies from the near contemporary two-decker to the modern critical study: and such personalities as Pitt, Wellington, Peel, Palmerston, Disraeli and Gladstone, quite apart from the giants of poetry and literature generally, are analysed time and time again as more evidence comes to light. In this epoch Great Britain was in a heroic mood, exulting in international supremacy while her thinkers constructed a new order of society from the destructive theories which had originated with the French Revolution. But it was also the epoch of the middle-class: the squirearchy, which it replaced, would better have preserved its privileges by suppressing Stephenson and Watt than by voting against the Reform Bill. Once urbanisation and industrialisation took over, the classical order was gone for ever. Yet in the wealth of research which illuminates these developments fiscal history has been largely neglected; although reforms in taxation underwrote, to 1815, the victory over Napoleon, from 1842, the triumph of Free Trade and to 1895, Victorian prosperity generally.

When Pitt rose on December 3, 1798, acting as his own Chancellor of the Exchequer, to deliver his Budget speech, which only lasted an hour, he had to confess that he was a belated convert to income tax and that only now was he convinced that "a general tax shall be imposed on all leading branches of income." There would be some inequality: there would still be some evasion as there had been of the Assessed Taxes: but this was the nearest he could get to "a fair and equal contribution." Clearly the scheme did not amount to the dramatic break with the fiscal past which it has often been regarded: indeed the speech itself, generally agreed to be a model of clarity, elegance and precision was, at times, decidedly apologetic in tone. Yet there had always been in England a tradition of direct taxation if spasmodic in application: for instance land tax had intended to tax incomes, if frustrated in execution: and incessant campaigning by men of recognised authority went on throughout the eighteenth century for a tax on incomes. Finally the Triple Assessment of 1798, by affording relief by reference to annual income, so that the charge was on the lower of the full Triple Assessment or one-tenth of annual income, provided an immediate precedent for a direct tax on incomes of ten per cent.

In effect all Pitt did was to impose for the duration as a substantive tax the amount calculated on the basis of the "relief by reference to income" provisions of the Triple Assessment not only in its technical details but also in its rate, namely, a flat one-tenth on incomes of £200 and over. He also adopted, with minor amendments, the allowances for children and deductions in arriving at assessable income. Repairs, too, could be set against the annual value of real property, anticipating the maintenance relief abolished in 1964. Certainly the 1799 Act represented a considerable elaboration of the 1797 provisions, no doubt the result of administrative experience, and was remarkably sophisticated: but the 670 pages of the massive consolidation of 1970 have their true origin in the Act imposing the Triple Assessment of 1797, not the 1799 Act.

The administrative machinery was lifted directly from the land tax and so displayed that peculiarly English combination of central control and local executive power which still characterises it. It was deliberate policy on Pitt's part for securing a measure of consent to leave considerable discretionary power to the General Commissioners and Commercial Commissioners as a sop to the mercantile community's demands for secrecy. The bureaucratic side was represented by the Commissioners for the Affairs of the Taxes, the Auditor's Office to deal with collection and the local surveyor who could lay before his Commissioners "such grounds of doubt as may occur to him on the fairness of the rate at which a party may have assessed himself", a proposal which Parliament resisted violently despite the fact that the day to day executive power was in the hands of the Commissioners, their clerks and their assessors. Only a general return of income was called for simply declaring that the taxpayer was willing to pay a certain sum which he affirmed to be not less than a tenth of his income.

Pitt's income tax was not a success. The first year's yield, despite the elaborate estimate of £10 million, was in fact under £6 million. The cautious estimate of £7 million for 1800 was again unfulfilled with a yield again under £6 million. The 1801 estimate seemed realistic at £6 million but now the yield had fallen to under £5 million. These statistics were hardly surprising. As the local Commissioners reported, they had not the staff to examine many of the general returns, nor were there sufficient surveyors to inspect particular returns even if called for although there was an increase in their complement of "99 at £90 each" in 1800. Reductions and allowances were wide open to abuse by unscrupulous taxpayers. Thirdly, the Commercial Commissioners handled their fellows gently: Pitt had estimated profits from domestic trade and industry at a modest £28 million and calculated the yield therefore at £2.8 million: the return of profits was barely £6 million. It was, then, a temporary tax, a backward-looking tax in its reliance on the provisions of the Triple Assessment, still subject to what Pitt had bitterly termed "shameful evasions or rather scandalous frauds" and not really as inquisitorial as its detractors had assumed: it is hard to visualise any requirement less inquisitorial than that of making a general return of income under the 1799 Act. But although in this respect it was the last gasp of eighteenth century voluntaryism, it was also the climax of another eighteenth century trend away from indirect taxation however tentative and however socially dangerous importing equity might seem in Pitt's eyes. But even so it was he who in those few short winter days of 1798 persuaded Parliament and public to accept a direct tax on income and a radical change in the fiscal scene.

In February 1801 Pitt resigned over the Catholic Emancipation issue: Addington, his successor, at last concluded the long drawn out peace negotiations with France in march 1802: and when he introduced his Budget in the following month he was forced to repeal Pitt's income tax, not only on account of its unpopularity but because of keeping faith with the promise that it was a war tax exclusively. However Addington was taking no chances, and soon after his Budget, was requesting the Revenue authorities to prepare plans for a general consolidation and revision of all the duties under their care.

Hostilities recommenced in May 1803, and Addington's Budget of that June included what he tactfully called "a separate tax on property", but at only half Pitt's rate: it was, although passed by Parliament under the title of the Property Duty Act, in fact income tax by the back door and, despite the suspicions it aroused, greeted with much less hostility than its predecessor. Its importance, however, rests on its introduction into the taxation system of two basic changes, both of which have survived to this day. The first was the requirement for particular returns of income from particular sources instead of the lump sum demanded in the 1799 Act which was an elaboration of the schedular system also found in Louis XIV's dixième. The second was the vital principle of deduction of tax at source which was set out in section 208 of the 1803 Act in phraseology incorporated, virtually unchanged, in 1952,ss. 169 and 170. At first this principle was not extended to Schedule C but in 1806 when the change was effected the charge rose from just under £12 million in 1803 to £20 million in 1806. By this time Pitt had taken over from Addington but so successful had the new system proved itself in doubling the efficiency of the tax despite the halving of the rate that Pitt adopted it virtually unchanged.

Addington has been hardly used by historians: his political record was one of undistinguished probity but in his period as Chancellor of the Exchequer he was responsible for two taxation principles of dramatic efficiency and durability. Certainly he did not originate them: but doubtless in his discussions with the Revenue Department he would have considered the schedular system since it was based on the sub-divisions in the particular form of return which the 1799 Act called for if the general return was challenged. As for the principle of deduction of tax at source, this was a combination of two circumstances; Addington's profound knowledge of taxation history and the experience of his officials. Their precedents stemmed from the revived land tax of 1688 not only for deducting and retaining tax which had been permitted since the fourteenth century but for deducting tax at source to be paid over to the Revenue.

The 1806 Income Tax Act settled the final shape of the tax for the next decade. It was simplified to the extent of dropping exemption and abatement for small incomes to £50, repairs allowance for property and relief for children: the rate, however, was doubled to Pitt's old figure of ten per cent. Thenceforward even the most casual references to income tax occur rarely in Hansard until the end of its wartime life. By February 1815, as Napoleon had been in exile for a year, repeal was in the air: but with his escape the yield rose to a patriotic £16 millions. This was its final contribution: for when the Chancellor of the Exchequer, Vansittart, announced in his

"Financial Exposition" of February 1816 that he proposed to continue the property tax while reducing it to half-rate, he was met with a storm of protests and petitions distinguished more by vehemene than by logic. The debates raged through February until 18 March when Vansittart made a last-ditch defence and managed to contain the majority for repeal to a mere thirty-seven votes. So ended, for the time being, Pitt's bold experiment reinforced by Addington's brilliant amendments. But the lesson that an income tax could be made to work, that there was a department capable of operating it, and that the bogey of interference was more apparent than real was not forgotten: the old, casual, quota-based system of direct taxation of tenths and fifteenths, grants, aids and subsidies was gone for ever.

There is an ironic coda to the 1816 repeal of income tax. At the temporary repeal of 1802 the Commissioners immediately ordered the destruction of all records of the tax which were to be collected, cut into pieces with large stationer's shears, conveyed to a paper manufacturer and there, under the eyes of a Commissioner, be reduced to pulp. It was understood that the 1802–1815 documents were similarly destroyed: indeed there is a legend that some were joyfully incinerated in Old Palace Yard, Westminster. But duplicates of the land and assessed taxes had always been sent to the King's Remembrancer and the same procedure was automatically applied to the income tax records: and at some unknown date they were bundled into sacks and sent to the Public Record Office where they lay undisturbed until 1932. The Deputy Auditor, whose office windows overlooked the scene of the bonfire, must have smiled sardonically at the thought of the duplicates safe in the Exchequer Court.

Fortunately a drop of £16 million in revenue could be cushioned by the increased yield from customs and excise, still the mainstay of the national income: and even with the cost of government mounting, the National Debt at £861 millions and the problems arising from the return to the gold standard in 1819, there was an impressive reduction in tariffs during the 1820s, including a graded set of corn law duties, a tax dating from the seventeenth century, in 1828. Direct taxation, on the other hand, lacked any organising intelligence and was becoming a makeshift collection of levies of varying efficiency, yield and convenience with the one common factor of evasion. There were taxes on specific professions and trades, from solicitors to hawkers, imposed by means of certificates: there were taxes "on persons providing the means of locomotion" from coaches to railways. These, however, were not as productive as legacy duty and probate duty which, although not progressive and levied at a fairly generous rate, jointly raised about £2 million by the late 1820s, those on insurances which yielded nearly £1 million and stamp duties which showed a steady annual rise.

There remained the assessed taxes, containing almost as many complications as all the foregoing classes combined, levied under some sixty different Acts, interpreted by two thousand judicial decisions, and including taxes on menservants, saddle, carriage- and racehorses, game certificates, hair powder, dogs and armorial bearings. The principal contributors to the yield of the assessed taxes were, however the window tax and the inhabited house duty, a tax originally imposed on the rack rental of private houses at a rate as high as 33 per cent, which jointly produced nearly £3 million in 1815. Progressive exemptions, however, diminished the yield so that by 1834 Althorp's considerable Budget surplus enabled him to abolish the I.H.D. altogether although window tax was the favourite candidate.

Pressure for relief was also affecting indirect taxation and the period also saw a movement for repeal of the salt tax. There was a parliamentary Committee of Enquiry in 1818 and the general conclusion was that "a repeal of the salt duties would be productive of the greatest and most important advantages to all descriptions of persons in this kingdom". The problem which confronted the government, as always in any lobby for repeal, was how to replace the consequent deficiency in the revenue. Agricultural distress and reductions in wages stimulated the demand for reductions in taxation, although the ministerial attitude was that all round decreases were preferable to specific abolitions. Finally the weight of public opinion, expressed by petitions, prevailed: in 1822 it was finally proposed, "despite the solicitations of the collectors of it" that the tax should expire in 1825.

Such piecemeal reforms illustrate that, although the financial scene was still dominated by Adam Smith, and his opposition to taxes on income as "arbitrary and uncertain", the simplicity of his classical theories was becoming increasingly irrelevant to contemporary circumstances. A French historian, mindful of the precise organisation of his country, summed up the England of this period as "a disorderly society": the fiscal system was equally so. Its two virtues were that it worked and that in a boom period there could even be remissions thanks to increased consumption.

For a time all went well as direct taxes continued to pay their way and the yield of indirect levies steadily mounted. The financial crisis of 1825, however, enforced the inevitable policy of economy since there was no surplus and no national propensity for new taxation. In fact more than one association was formed in this period for the purpose of refusing to pay any taxes at all. By the 'thirties, however, it had been found possible to initiate a quasi-free trade programme. 1834 was probably the high water-mark of Whig finance with further remissions to absorb a surplus of over £1,500,000: but the four years from 1835 saw a series of deficits created by indiscriminate repeal. The appointment of Baring, from the famous banking family, as Chancellor came too late and by 1841 Peel was saying of him: "Can there be a more lamentable picture than that of a Chancellor of the Exchequer seated on an empty chest, by the pool of bottomless deficiency, fishing for a budget?" The laissez-faire theories derived from Adam Smith and the popular "ignorant impatience of taxation" had produced a policy of fiscal expediency which had pushed the country to the verge of bankruptcy.

Fortunately, ever since the repeal of income tax, there had been a subterranean movement towards its restoration. Ricardo, the most influential of the early nineteenth century economists had come out strongly in favour of it: so had the so-called "Manchester" school of economists. Perhaps the most significant piece of advocacy was "Observations and Suggestions with a view to the Substitution of an Income or Property Tax for the Present Taxes." It was published in 1831 but a draft might well have been available to Peel when he was discussing income tax with the Treasury in 1830 and 1831. For its author was well-known in fiscal circles as Benjamin Sayer, a senior Revenue official and an exceptionally hard worker although suffering from indifferent health. The book was also quoted with approval in the fiscal debates of the period. Select Committees to look into a general revision of taxation were proposed in 1830 and 1833, the opposition to which was led by Peel: but he entered a caveat that "he would not say that circumstances might not arise in war, or even in peace, to justify an income tax". The question was raised again both in 1835 and 1836 to receive the old argument of no income tax in peacetime for the ingenious reason that there would be no such tax to fall back on in wartime. "No: let indirect taxation be the source of your revenue in peace and leave direct taxation in the shape of a property tax for the advent of war."

Peel was the Prime Minister who, more than any other in the nineteenth century except perhaps Palmerston, exemplified Bagehot's dictum that "a constitutional statesman is a man of common opinions and uncommon abilities". He was fully aware that the originally passionate hostility to income tax had largely abated: this fact was immediately relevant in view of the current political and

A Short History of Taxation

economic scene in 1842, a period of confusion and darkness. Both the Anti-Corn Law League and the Chartists had their own remedies for the crisis. The genius of Peel lay in his ability to exploit the waning antipathy to income tax by reintroducing it to subsidise a free trade policy which would simultaneously satisfy the protagonists of the Free Trade movement and, by lowering the cost of living, pacify the workers left behind in industrial progress who made up the majority of the Chartist movement.

When he rose to present his Budget the secret had been well kept, although suspicions were aroused since, like Pitt, he insisted on making the introduction himself. There was a deficiency of nearly £5 million which was symptomatic of a chronic condition which had existed over the past seven or eight years: despite this he was not proposing any additional duty on "great articles of consumption" since such a levy had not proved as elastic as an increase on what he termed ominously as taxes on a subject "analagous to property". Then came the dramatic announcement. "I propose that, for a time to be limited, the income of this country should be called upon to contribute a certain sum ... not exceeding 7d. in the pound ... for the purpose of not only supplying the deficiency in the revenue, but of enabling me with confidence and satisfaction to propose great commercial reforms, which will afford a hope of reviving commerce and such an improvement in the manufacturing interest as will react on every other interest in the country: and, by diminishing the prices of articles of consumption and the cost of living will, in a pecuniary point of view compensate you for your present sacrifices ..." He then gave a brief history of the tax, indicated that he was preparing a streamlined version without allowances, exempting all incomes under £150, and charging the occupation of land at only one half the rental: the yield he estimated at £3.7 millions. Together with the increases in indirect taxation he could command a surplus of nearly £2 millions.

His plans for dealing with this surplus were already formulated. "I propose to apply it in a manner which I think will be most consonant with public feeling and opinion by making great improvements in the commercial tariff of England and to abate the duties on some great articles of consumption." The eighteenth century Customs Acts had scheduled over two thousand dutiable articles. Peel's new tariff had only twenty heads and no less than seven hundred and fifty articles were affected. The immediate reaction of the House was to oppose: but Peel conducted a remarkable public relations exercise by enlisting the aid of the young Queen who he was able to announce had expressed "her determination that her own income should be subjected to a similar charge." The loud and prolonged cheers which greeted this royal beneficence and the smiling alacrity with which Victoria was said to be contributing her sevenpence camouflaged her mentor, Lord Melbourne's, advice that she was throwing away her money and her prerogative, according to which she was constitutionally exempt from paying income tax; and in fact she agreed to accept liability only with great reluctance. This was true of the country in general: but, after a series of protracted debates, the Bill was passed on June 22, 1842 in virtually the same form as it had been laid before the House four months before.

Peel's reintroduction of income tax as the permanent feature of the fiscal system it became was a matter of fiscal accident rather than fiscal design. The Income Tax Act of 1842 was, with minor modifications, virtually a reprint of the 1806 Act. He did not concentrate much attention, therefore, on the form of the income tax legislation he put forward: in fact, of a speech of fiftyeight columns, he devoted basically only three to the reimposition of income tax. Finally he did sincerely believe that the tax, in his own words, could be levied "for a time to be limited." It was revived not for its intrinsic merits as a tax but as means for simplifying and reducing the tariff. Peel's weakness, common to all pragmatists was that he confused a point scored in debate with a truth discovered in argument: few Members saw through his strategy: although one commented: "I will never consent to an income tax wrung from the people for the purpose of speculating in free trade". Peel never intended a revolution in direct taxation or he would not have looked backwards to 1806: he was making the first step towards the repeal of the Corn Laws and, later, towards the imperial and industrialised Britain of the latter half of the nineteenth century.

The immediate effects of the 1842 Budget were disappointing. The yield of income tax would have shown an excess of £1 million plus over the estimate had not, by a technical blunder, the Exchequer got only a half-year's revenue in the current financial year: indirect taxation also showed a true shortfall from the estimate with a deficit of over £2 million. But trade began to pick up and there were two good harvests in succession. By 1844 the yield of taxation had so increased that a surplus of £2 million was realised and the duties on glass, vinegar, currants, coffee and wool were either reduced or abolished.

In 1845 Peel again introduced the Budget: he was now proposing to continue income tax for a second three-year period: without it, by 1846–7 he forecast another deficiency: with it, the fiscal foundations of the country would be securely based. He was still using the tax "not for the purpose of providing supplies for the year, but distinctly for the purpose of enabling us to make this great experiment of reducing other taxes". The surplus of £3.5 million would be devoted to the remitting of indirect taxation; sugar duties were reduced, 430 articles were removed from the tariff and all the remaining export duties were abolished. Excise lost nearly that amount by the repeal of the auction and glass duties. A new fiscal principle was emerging of absolutely repealing instead of merely reducing duties.

But the landed interest was beginning to look askance at a policy from which it derived no apparent benefits; and this suspicion deepened into certainty when the Budget of 1846 proposed at long last the repeal of the corn duties: this was indeed the most spectacular part of the Bill: but in addition customs duties, to the extent of over £1 million, were remitted. The general intention was to stabilise the rate on most manufactured articles as near 10 per cent as possible.

Despite all these remissions customs, excise, stamp duties and direct taxation had a combined yield of almost £400,000 more in 1847 than in 1842; while on customs and excise alone the drop in yield was less than £50,000. The principal reason was the remarkable expansion in British trade which was to continue at least to the end of the century despite the periodic commercial crises of which arose from over-investment in the new railways both here and in the United States.

Just as the decade in fiscal history from 1842 to 1852 is dominated by the name of Peel, so the years from 1853 to 1866 are similarly dominated by the name of Gladstone. Both the men and their periods are comparable, especially in the extension of the free trade programme and the use of income tax as a means for achieving this. Gladstone began his régime as Chancelor of the Exchequer in 1853 with a further round of customs revisions. But it was in 1860 that "the noble work of commercial reform" was completed by him, leaving finally a handful of duties only and those specifically for revenue purposes, to balance a severely controlled expenditure.

There were two dominant factors of the fiscal scene in 1860: the first was the conclusion of the Anglo-French Treaty granting mutual trading concessions and the second the falling-in of the long-dated stock which put some £2 millions at Gladstone's disposal. This fortunate conjunction would enable him to fulfil his ambition "to do something for trade and for the masses": and this meant, in his own words "a sweep, summary, entire and absolute, of the duty on what are known as manufactured goods from the face of the British tariff".

Salt, gloves, watches and artificial flowers were made free from duty: as also were such foods as butter, cheese, eggs, oranges and nuts together with such fats as tallow. Only fourteen revenue-raisers remained: there were five, namely spirits, sugar, tea, tobacco and wine each yielding between £1 million to £6 million: there were four each yielding between £200,000 to £1 million, coffee, cocoa, currants and timber: the balance, chicory, figs, hops, pepper and raisins raised between £20,000 and £200,000 each. Excise raised some £20 millions, principally from spirits and malt; so that the yield of indirect taxation averaged over the period around £45 million.

The attitude of both Peel and Gladstone to indirect taxation was severely pragmatic: the latter had, however, carefully considered the dilemma of the balance which he thought should be kept between direct and indirect taxation. It was on this problem that he had delivered his famous pronouncement on the charms of the two sisters, Necessity and Invention, as he sub-titled the two branches of taxation, to whom he was forced to pay court, and to whose respective fascinations he was equally susceptible. Thus more or less equal demands were made on both: and this balance was accepted as normal.

From the 'sixties the doctrine of Free Trade was not seriously challenged for some twenty years, but on the Continent the movement died down soon after the Anglo-French treaty of 1860. Free Traders had argued that international commerce fostered international co-operation, but with the advent of aggressive nationalism governments were more impressed with the fiscal advantages of urban populations and the strategic virtues of flourishing metallurgical and engineering industries: in the end tariffs were met with tariffs as the high ideals of Free Trade shaded off into the emotional appeal of neo-Protectionism and Fair Trade at the close of the century.

The rationalisation of indirect taxation was accompanied by reforms in organisation. The transfer of some duties to the Customs and the wholesale repeal of other Excise duties stimulated staffing economies: in 1849 therefore the Excise, Assessed Taxes and the Stamp Duties offices were amalgamated: Customs, however, re-mained independent. In the event there were manpower savings at the higher levels: Collectors of Excise were appointed Receivers of Taxes and Distributors of Stamps: and a commission of enquiry into Customs management in 1848 recommended a reduction in the number of Customs commissioners to seven and that "such appointments ought to be made with a scrupulous regard to the possession of the requisite qualifications"; that is, professionalism was taking over from nepotism.

Indirect taxation was a traditional, accepted and familiar fiscal weapon: successive Chancellors, for at least two centuries, had found it easy to manipulate its incidence, to modify its pressure and to estimate its product. But income tax was a far less manageable levy: it was comparatively new, unpopular and ostensibly existed only on sufferance to buttress the current free trade programme: in addition its yield was unpredictable since distorted by various forms of evasion ranging from simple omissions of income to the presentation of fraudulent accounts. Even so every Chancellor from 1842 was faced with the awkward necessity of defining his attitude towards it, an exercise attended with varying success and degrees of honesty.

Lord John Russell, when he took over from Peel in 1848, proposed the continuation of income tax for a further five years; finally he could only renew the tax at 7d. for three years. Peel's fiscal dominance was clearly lacking: for the first time there were hints of dissatisfaction with the uniform incidence of income tax, summarised by Cobden. "If a distinction were made between permanent and ,precarious incomes, if a graduation of duty were established, you would have no remonstrances." It was the possibility of introducing these two reforms which was to occupy the thoughts and energies of fiscal reformers past the end of the century.

Experts both inside and outside the House were able to express their opinion to the Hume Committee in 1851, appointed to "enquire into the present mode of assessing and collecting the Income and Property Tax and whether any other mode of levying the same, so as to render the Tax more equitable, can be adopted." Numerous witnesses were examined whose evidence is embalmed in two volumes but no final recommendations were made: "there was not sufficient time for discussing and preparing a report that could do justice to this complicated subject." The witnesses were, on the whole, conservative, and since, over the decade of its revival, income tax was only providing about 10 per cent of the revenue which put it well behind customs and excise at 38 per cent and 25 per cent respectively, they had every excuse for avoiding a considered judgment on a tax which seemed neither vital nor permanent. Practicability was the test of a good tax: differentiation i.e. distinguishing between earned and unearned income, was regarded as inequitable and unworkable: graduation was suspect as redistributive and, as such, unacceptable. Parliament echoed the general sense of the Committee being anxious to retain the tax, if at all, as it stood. Disraeli's second Budget confirmed this: his tentative steps towards differentiation were blocked by the massed ranks of the financial experts of the day, and the Government fell before the end of the year.

Gladstone followed with his two "great" Budgets of 1853 and 1860. His speech on the first included a three-hour, forty-column dissertation on income tax: his conclusion was that it remained a convenience tax, suitable for continuing Peel's policy of remission "but not well adapted for a permanent portion of your fiscal system". He proposed its continuation for a total period of seven years at reducing rates so that at April 5, 1860, "the Income Tax will expire". It was, however, essential for the Crimean War and provided tolerable surpluses due to the buoyancy of the revenue; and although to the reformers a flat-rate income tax "was that obnoxious and most mischievous impost" it had proved to have the specific virtue of providing an elastic element in the Budget.

In 1860, however, Gladstone was unable to redeem his pledge of seven years before. Deeply conscious as he was of "reaching an important epoch in British finance" the deficiency he was faced with forced him to increase its rate by 1d. instead of repealing. He could muster plenty of support in the long debates which followed but he met an almost equal amount of criticism. Financial experts stressed the essential point that something definite should be done about income tax: it was not satisfactory to leave it in its current ambivalent position.

Historians and economists have eulogised Gladstone as a fiscal expert ever since the "financial landmark" of the 1853 Budget but this assessment is hardly justified by an analysis of his Budgets, for he was strangely misguided in his attitude towards income tax in assuming it could be repealed without provision against further remissions in indirect taxation and against fresh additions to national expenditure especially on the armed forces. He was more obstinate than logical in opposing differentiation when he declared it "tended to communism" and was "dangerous to property". He could not deploy the imagination which Disraeli had shown in his fiscal proposals or share his conviction that income tax was here to stay. A moral objection was its encouragement of evasion: and thus, nourishing the illusion of extinction and the charge of corruption, he never precisely defined his attitude towards it or agreed to its reform. Certainly he brought both eloquence and authority to his great office which had languished too long in the hands of nonentities. Not a great fiscal innovator, he was certainly a supreme fiscal publicist; although, like many publicists he fell victim to his own expertise in how to encourage hopes without actually making promises. It might be argued that the Hubbard Committee of 1863 justified Gladstone's reservations since it found that differentiation did not afford "a basis for a practicable and equitable readjustment of the income tax", that "danger and ill-consequences were to be apprehended from an attempt to unsettle the present basis of the tax", and therefore that they had no suggestions for its amendment. But the Committee was in fact packed with Gladstone's nominees and the master himself attended twelve out of the nineteen sessions.

Meanwhile, under pressure of war and the weight of theoretical discussions including two Committees, if not two agreed Reports, both the central and local administration of income tax were settling down. Charles Pressly, the Board's Chairman, (who eventually retired on a record full salary as pension) and his officials, were developing a strong sense of responsibility and a marked appreciation of their increasingly technical problems: their first Report, published in 1857, listed the duties controlled comprising excise, stamps, probate, legacy and succession duty, as well as income tax, "the most important of all duties under our management" as well as the assessed taxes and house duty, substituted for window duty in 1851; it also made the usual compalints about evasion. In 1862 the "Chief Inspection Department" was created with Edward Hyde as the first Chief Inspector: he had under him a staff of 210 Surveyors (later Inspectors) of Taxes, of six different grades, ranging in salary from the Assistant with a maximum salary of £150 to the Senior Surveyor, of whom there were only 25, with a maximum salary of £450. The local organisation was still very much in the hands of the General Commissioners and their Clerk who made assessments, heard appeals and appointed Collectors, a duty the Board coveted. But the most significant feature of the Reports is the emergence of the Surveyor as the prototype of the modern government servant, now appointed through departmental examinations, responsible for an increasing amount of tax and "not surpassed by any public servants in the same class in intelligence and judgment, in the discharge of very troublesome and invidious functions," or so the Board thought.

In the thirty years to 1894 there were two notable Budgets divided by a period roughly covering the Tory government of 1874–1880 when income tax reached its lowest ebb. During that time income tax achieved a qualified acceptance, qualified in the reformers' eyes by the hope of introducing differentiation and graduation and qualified in the traditionalists' eyes by the hope, growing ever fainter, of total abolition. This equivocal position of what had become the most important balancing item in the revenue gave successive Chancellors less room for manoeuvre than they might have hoped for if Parliament could have made up its mind about the "hated impost". So from 1863 to 1869 the Chancellor's approach to his annual fiscal task was inevitably tentative: and provided there was a surplus the methods by which it was achieved were not debated too closely. In any case profits, wages and consumption were buoyant and increases in revenue came naturally with increases in the gross national product.

But a decided recession in 1869 placed Lowe, the Chancellor, in a position which he described as "possessing almost every element of ill-luck". He might have attempted a radical reform of income tax but he lacked the resolution and, it must be admitted, the support of public opinion. Instead, by accelerating the payment of the tax, he converted his deficiency into a surplus without prejudicing the revenue of future years. But still no definite view was taken of the tax itself, of its retention or abolition: and Lowe's Budget, ingenious though it was, seems more an exercise in fiscal mechanics than fiscal philosophy.

In fact for a few years in the 'seventies, abolition, with the rate at 2d. in 1874, seemed almost realisable: and the basic reason why this was not achieved lay in the simple reason that it seemed hardly worth the trouble. Its low rates, its limited incidence, its comparative insignificance by the side of customs and excise gave it a negligible impact on the revenue and the nation at large. Its innocuousness saved it: the main objection was not the amount of tax it imposed but the inconvenience of paying it at all.

But it was not until Harcourt's Budget of 1894 that any reflection of the controversies over differentiation and graduation began to emerge. This was the Budget which started with the intention of reforming death duties which were sub-divided into five classes, probate, account, estate, legacy and succession and graduating income tax: but in the end the Chancellor had to settle for amalgamating the five duties under the generic title of Estate Duty and graduating its rate from 1 per cent up to £5000, to 8 per cent where over £1 million. It is doubtful whether he realised the full significance of his proposals which he forced through the House in three months of bitter debate and a record two thousand columns of Hansard, since he regarded graduation not as a fiscal tenet but more as a principle of liberal finance. Even so, his tentative introduction of that limited

129

measure finally exorcised the ghost of Gladstone from Somerset House.

Income tax had taken some sixty years to come of age. Introduced by Pitt and improved by Addington, its revival, after a gap from 1816 to 1842, by Peel was deliberately to balance the loss of revenue from the long process of tariff reform: and, during the Gladstone era, it was a fiscal convenience not a fiscal doctrine. Until 1894 its only real concession to equity was a comparatively high tax threshold. Fortunately the combination of amateur jurisdiction and professional administration had forged a consent based on tolerance if not absolute acceptability. It is easy to antedate modern income tax and to forget that well within living memory its yield, at £15 millions, hardly compared with customs of £20 millions and excise of £25 millions, both of which were more easily policed: that an engagingly cavalier attitude was taken to returns of income: and that the conception of a personal income tax was only just emerging since three-quarters was paid by deduction. In fact, as the new century drew nearer, income tax, after existing on sufferance could hardly do more than congratulate itself on survival.

Chapter IX

Modern Taxation in Peace and War 1896–1980

This final chapter must inevitably be more ragged and abrupt than its predecessors since the ends of so many twentieth century developments in politics, economics, science and culture have yet to work themselves out. It is possible however to sub-divide the past eighty years or so into three periods which, whilst shading off into each other, yet possess distinctive features. The first is perhaps the most clearly defined, the twenty years to 1914 when the State hardly intruded in the life of the average man, when war still had overtones of chivalry, when there were no tariffs and when taxation mulcted the national income of a modest five per cent. The impact of World War I transformed the individual into a citizen: and the grasp of the State gradually tightened during the second period ending in 1939 when the pace of rearmament dispelled the cold war between rich and poor and the shadow of unemployment which had haunted the country since the Armistice. Lastly, the generation from 1945 saw a new industrial revolution from the old natural staples of wool and cotton to the new man-made fibres, from heavy engineering to electronics, from coal to oil. It also saw the birth of the welfare state. But one of the most radical changes was in taxation. As Free Trade could not survive economic nationalism, indirect taxation again began to assume the complexities of the pre-Peel era: as for direct taxation, it had already emerged as part of the normal fiscal scene: for the extraordinary demands of war and welfare new direct taxes were imposed in the shape of excess profits levies or surtaxes on income. No sooner had these specific tasks been performed than direct taxation was called upon to undertake the more subtle and complex function of economic regulation. If the eighteenth century was the age of enlightenment and the nineteenth the age of industrialisation, the twentieth may well go down in history as the age of taxation.

By its very nature, indirect taxation aroused more political contention than direct. For instance, of the two issues of Imperial Preference and Protection, the former caused internal dissensions in the Conservative Party and the latter clearly divided Conservatives from Liberals. In addition the growing influence of Labour was consistently opposed to any extension of indirect taxation, basically because of its lack of discrimination between rich and poor, except for levies on luxuries. Apart from these political implications, the statistical history of indirect taxation showed a steadily increasing yield in peace-time and a spectacular upsurge during the war years. In 1901 Customs and Excise brought in some £32 million: before the end of World War I this had become £100 million: by 1945 it had multiplied tenfold, and this with the addition only of one new tax, purchase tax.

There was not a great deal of administrative change apart from one most important development introduced by the Finance Act 1908 which had its roots far back in the previous century. As early as 1862 the possible amalgamation of the Inland Revenue and the Customs had been considered but both Gladstone and the Board of Inland Revenue had opposed it. Seven years later the Ridley Commission had recommended that amalgamation was inexpedient in spite of Gladstone's evidence that he now thought the time was ripe. There followed a period of jockeying for position but by 1899 the Chairman of the Board of Inland Revenue was reporting that an amalgamation of Customs and Excise was the more practical proposition, although he warned that there were serious disadvantages. In 1908, however, Asquith reached the conclusion that these disadvantages were out-weighed by considerations of "administration, economy and efficiency" and it was decided by Order in Council that the transfer of Excise from the Board of Inland Revenue to Customs should take place on 3 December 1909 and the integrated services soon began to work smoothly together. It was just as well: new challenges presented themselves such as the pioneer flight of Blériot whose plane Customs ingeniously categorised as a yacht for quarantine purposes, observing presciently that the arrival of aircraft might need serious considera-tion so that "no revenue should be lost by their indiscriminate landing". Of more immediate relevance was the growing popularity of the motor car which gave rise in 1909 to the first imposition of motor spirit duty at 3d per gallon when the customer paid a mere 6d per gallon: the initial yield of this future money-spinner was only a modest £312,881. On the duties in general, it was remarkable that the first financial year after amalgamation the amounts paid into the Exchequer by the two sections were almost equal, customs netting £30.123 million and excise £30.542 million: the former had tobacco and tea as best payers, the latter spirits and beer.

Two main themes provide continuity in the fiscal success story of Customs and Excise which itself was basically the result of a steady increase, with the occasional pause, in earnings, especially those of the manual worker. Firstly there was the gradual erosion of the once sacrosanct doctrine of Free Trade which may be said to have come to its end in 1932 with the Import Duties Act of that year. This in effect was indirect taxation in its political guise when revenue-raising was relegated to second place. Secondly there was the speed with which taxation overtook most potentially dutiable new activities or products: petrol was already in the net to be followed shortly by cinema entertainment. This steady growth in subjects of charge accounted for the buoyancy of yield rather than new taxes which were rare and which arose either from pressure of war or political considerations.

The issue of Free Trade versus Protection was first raised by Joseph Chamberlain under the disarming title of 'imperial preference' although he coupled with this a belief in fiscal retaliation against foreign tariffs. A compromise that this latter policy should be considered by the Government offended the "taxation for revenue only" enthusiasts and failed to placate Chamberlain. This gave the Liberals the chance of unfurling their old Free Trade standard and the long Conservative domination closed in 1905. There was no difficulty about funding their social legislation in the pre-1914 period since it only represented one per cent of the national income and was amply covered by increases in tobacco and spirit duty.

It took a world war to make the first real breach in Free Trade with the McKenna import duties of 1915, as a result of which Customs and Excise receipts for the first time exceeded £100 million. But even so, when Baldwin made Protection a Conservative policy in 1923 the country decisively rejected it in the subsequent election which led to the first Labour government. It was not until after the crisis of 1931 and the virtual extinction of effective political opposition that the Conservatives were finally in a position to introduce the Import Duties Bill in 1932 which, as far as the Commonwealth was concerned, was tempered by the Ottawa Agreement of the same year.

These developments represented a radical break with traditional British policy but the twin arguments that tariffs represented a bargaining counter against discrimination and a mechanism for increasing or at least maintaining employment carried the day. In the event, however, the direct influence of protection was not significant. Certainly the improvement in the balance of payments position helped to create the right conditions for recovery. But no new industries were created: the younger industries, such as chemicals, had grown up under the shelter of the tariff protection policy of the 1920's: there were only a handful of industries where restriction of imports had immediately affected domestic production. The overall effect on employment and production was inconsiderable.

World War I inevitably pushed the political aspect of indirect taxation into the background again: and it was not until 30 October 1947 that the war-time alliances which had shaded into peace-time associations fostered the idea of a General Agreement on Tariffs and Trade by which the British rates of duty on many articles were reduced or "bound" against increase. This process was part of a move towards a European Customs Union to produce a greater tariff uniformity among the countries of Europe. Progress was renewed in 1950 when further reductions in some British tariffs were conceded. But the main work on the abolition of tariff barriers altogether was undertaken first by the formation of the European Economic Community by the Treaty of Rome in 1957, of which Britain was not a member, and then by the establishment, two years later, of the European Free Trade Association, to which Britain did subscribe and which led, in 1966, to the cancellation of Customs duty under the Import Duties Act of 1958 on goods of EFTA origin other than certain agricultural and fishery products.

Customs and Excise as a fiscal weapon showed an erratic yield in the 1920s after the massive war-time contribution. The depression of 1921, the short period while the McKenna Duties were in abeyance in 1924 and the General Strike of 1926 all had a marked effect and increases in the staple duties and the first imposition of a duty on hydrocarbon oil in 1928 nearly twenty years after petrol had first been taxed left revenue still lagging behind the estimate. It was not until after the crisis of 1929–1931 that the second Finance Act of 1931 achieved a net revenue surplus of a bare £2.2 million by increasing duties on beer, tobacco and hydrocarbon oils. This increase was continued in the following decade by the operation of the tariff, receipts topping £135 million in 1931–32, rising sharply to £180 in the two succeeding years, and levelling off at some £222 million in

1937–38. The best payers throughout the period continued to be spirits, sugar, tobacco, beer and hydrocarbon oils: other items were comparatively insignificant.

With the outbreak of World War II came an immediate and progressive increase in rates and a staggering advance in receipts which rose from £400 million in 1939 to over £1,000 million by the end of the war despite restrictions and rationing. There was, however, a completely new tax, purchase tax, brought into operation by the Purchase Tax (Commencement) Order 1940 levied on most consumer goods: it was soon to reach the £100 million mark. It is noteworthy that cost of collection in 1945 was a mere .55 per cent, and that staff had been run down to less than 10,000.

Since 1945 the yield of Customs and Excise both overall and globally remained at record levels: only in two years, 1949–50 and 1970–71, did receipts ever fall below those of the previous year. There was a consolidation exercise in 1952, when the Customs and Excise Act of that year repealed some 200 Acts passed during the previous century and a half. A year later the Committee to review the Department's organisation reported but recommended no radical alterations. In fact, until 1972, the principal new taxes during the period were those which covered virtually the whole field of organised gambling and which were completed by the general betting duty of 1966. But more important than the actual yield of indirect taxation or its all-pervasive nature was its capacity for being used as an instant economic regulator for decreasing domestic demand to improve the balance of payments position: for instance in 1951 purchase tax on consumer durables was doubled and in 1967 the 10 per cent. surcharge was incorporated in the substantive rates of duty applicable to all articles liable. The continued rise in receipts shows how much purchasing power was siphoned off in regulating exercises of this sort for by 1964–65 Customs and Excise contributed 42.7 per cent of total revenue. One final figure, which like so many in indirect taxation illuminates a whole sector of social change, was that by the 1970s the yield from hydrocarbon oil duty at last overtook that of tobacco which had held pride of place for a century. But the traditional distinction between indirect taxation in its political aspect and in its fiscal guise was blurred by the entry of this country into the Common Market on 1 January 1973 and the introduction of value added tax by the 1972 Finance Act. This was certainly a "political" tax in the sense that it was part of that process by which, after an agreed transitional period, the whole of the internal and external tax policy of the EEC was to be harmonised. But VAT was also an entirely new fiscal weapon, re-placing purchase tax and necessitating not only a re-education of the business world but the Customs and Excise establishment also. A major publicity campaign was mounted, involving the printing of 4½ million explanatory leaflets and the distribution of 1½ million VAT "packages" to all known businesses. Registration began in October 1972 and by April of the following year nearly one million businesses had been registered. And as the volume of consumer spending rises, indirect taxation finds itself poised between managing its domestic policies alone and participating in the wider international scene. It is a melancholy thought that currently the shining hopes of political and economic unification in a community of Europe have degenerated into nationalistic struggles for immediate advantages.

Whatever the additions, alterations or improvements to indirect taxation, as far as customs and excise were concerned they remained instantly recognisable as legitimate descendants of their seventeenth and eighteenth century ancestors. The position was very different with income tax, the acceptance of which had pursued an erratic course until the 1870s and which, even on the eve of the twentieth century, was a simple type of levy, simply applied, "the latest auto-matic invention", as one ex-Chancellor described it; "put a penny in the slot and the thing is done". 1899 and the Boer War can be regarded as the watershed when the rate of income tax broke the shilling barrier and the Budget two years later estimated a larger revenue for the first time from direct as against indirect taxation. In addition there was now an intense interest, as there had been soon after the tax was introduced, in the reform of the tax itself which, through discussions on differences between earned and unearned income and graduating rates, had been gradually building up over the period.

The advocates of differentiation at first confined themselves to what they considered to be administrative abuses in taxation prac-tice, blossoming out in 1891 with a proposal for "a Committee to enquire into the Income Tax": opponents, however, mounted the usual defence that reform was not a practical proposition when two Committees had found against it: and on the issue of differentiation itself, there would be an inequitable amount of relief to the higher ranges of earned income as against the lower levels of investment income. After this rebuff, the differentiation campaign faded for a time into the background.

Graduation now began to force the pace of reform. Originally tarred with the Chartist brush, its early advocates made little headway. It was not until Joseph Chamberlain's Radical Programme of 1885 came out strongly for graduation that, reinforced by the best contemporary fiscal historians, and the famous Harcourt Budget of 1894, it was adopted by contemporary economists. Not that fiscal opinion was wholly unanimous: but more formidable was the opposition of the Board itself, a member of which published a pamphlet resisting any change in the current system, and arguing that a scale graduated from 1s. to 2s. on incomes over £5,000 would only yield an additional £3 million. For this comparatively trivial amount, as Austen Chamberlain put it, "the income tax is ruined as a great engine for procuring revenue: and if you superimpose on an assessment at the source a further assessment in the case of wealthy people for the purpose of graduation, this will enormously increase the cost, will entail whole new machinery, will become excessively inquisitorial and will offend powerful interests. I do not think the House could devise a more ingenious way of making the income tax unpopular, ultimately involving its total repeal". But the reformers were not to be denied: the establishment excuse that two investigations within ten years had found no reforms advisable was wearing thin since it had been pointed out that they were not bona fide enquiries. That of 1851 was an abortive Committee in that it never reported: that of 1862 was appointed against the wish of the government and Gladstone, and had not a fair opportunity of enquiring properly into income tax. Although the Committee now proposed was to be departmental only, at least it was free to consider the current vexed topics of both differentiation and graduation.

The Committee of 1906 was chaired by the veteran finance expert Sir Charles Dilke: its terms of reference were simply "to enquire into, and report upon the practicability of graduating the income tax and of differentiating, for the purpose of the tax, between permanent and precarious incomes." It took evidence for three months and reported in November. It found that differentiation could be introduced although the suggested mechanism was a variation in rate as between earned and unearned income rather than a fractional abatement for the former class. The real divergence of opinion appeared on the issue of graduation. The official view was still uncompromisingly hostile, but some expert statistical evidence seemed to show that the Board's figures could effectively be challenged. The Committee summarised its conclusion by finding that graduation was practicable especially in the form of a supertax, that differentiation was practicable also and that the abandonment of deduction of tax at source "would be disastrous".

The recommendations were swiftly translated into legislation. Asquith proposed in his second Budget that earned income not exceeding £2,000 should be charged at 9d. in the £ as against the standard 1s. charged on unearned income and by the end of the following year even the Board was forced to concede the reform had been "smooth and easy in its operation". When he become Prime Minister he was still mindful of the unfinished business of graduation: and he gave unswerving support to his Chancellor, Lloyd George, when he introduced in 1909 the type of supertax which the Dilke Committee had recommended: in its final form it was fixed at 6d. in the £ on all incomes over £5,000 "upon the amount by which such incomes exceed £3,000". This, together with increases in the rates of tax and a concession in the form of a child allowance resurrected from Pitt, formed the famous "1909 war Budget against Poverty" which sparked off a two-year domestic constitutional crisis: although, contrary to popular legend, it was not the supertax which caused the most vehement opposition but the tax on land values since it imposed a 20 per cent tax on increased land values with a complete change in the method of valuation.

The emphasis was now beginning to shift from taxation for revenue purposes to taxation with a definable social tinge. But the Budget of 1909 could hardly be stigmatised, as the Lords had it, as a class Budget. The Liberal attitude was succinctly defined by Asquith: "If we are to have social reform we must be ready to pay for it: and when I say we, I mean the whole nation, the working and consuming classes as well as the wealthier class of direct taxpayers". Lloyd George provided a faithful echo: "I have never had any sympathy with the idea that someone has got to be exempt because he is earning a small amount ..... The only principle I would lay down would be that they ought to contribute in proportion to their means." He may well have realised further that the poor were suffering in indirect taxation far more than in proportion to their taxability. But it was the Labour Party which was beginning to discern the faint glimmer of a welfare state far beyond the measured pace of Liberal social reform: and although Snowden, the official Labour Party spokesman on financial affairs (perhaps because he had once worked in the Collector of Taxes' office), welcomed the 1909 Budget as the first to grapple with the problem of wealth and poverty, his basic argument was pure socialism – "that the taxation of the rich is really a payment which has been made by the poor who have been exploited". But problems of equity, reform and even evasion vanished in the eventful days of July 1914 following the assassination at Sarajevo and the Chancellor's duty was transformed overnight from that of the regulator of national finance to the provider of revenue to meet ever-mounting expenditure.

The financing of World War I can be split into two sharply contrasting periods. There was no attempt at first to put taxation on a truly war basis, although there was an all-round increase in rates in the November 1914 Budget: but this was effective for only a third of the year; and in the second Budget of May 1915 no new taxation at all was imposed. Before then, however, Lloyd Geroge had been translated to the Ministry of Munitions, and his successor, Reginald McKenna, an ex-banker, was forced to meet the challenge of daily expenditure on the £4.5 million mark. The Budget (1915) by which he did so ushered in the second period of war taxation. Income tax was raised to an unprecedented 3s.6d. in the £, supertax could reach an astronomical 6s.10d. and, a radical departure, wages were to be taxed by quarterly assessment made by the Surveyor (Inspector). The traditionalists were up in arms at this extension of bureaucratic power, but the original income tax scheme was never designed for weekly wage earners. In addition an Excess Profits Duty was imposed at 50 per cent on profits earned over a pre-war standard: retained until 1921, it accounted for no less than 25 per cent of the total tax revenue during the period.

By the end of the war income tax had changed out of all recognition. No longer was it the simple Victorian mechanism with a uniform rate of pence in the pound. It was now a much more complex apparatus, admitting both differentiation in the form of an earned income relief, and graduation in the shape of a supertax, with the income tax rate at 6s. and the maximum supertax at 4s.6d. A limited range of personal releifs had also been introduced and, for industry, an embryonic system of capital allowances. The most remarkable change, however, was in yield from some £34 millions pre-war to nearly £585 millions in 1918. Equally radical were the parallel changes in administration, with an ever-growing wealth of judicial dicta. Day-to-day control now resided in the tax district not the General Commissioners' office: as Snowden put it: "Anybody who knows anything about the working of the income tax laws knows that 99 per cent of the disputes in regard to income tax are now settled by the Surveyor of Taxes ...... The real work is now being done by the Surveyors of Taxes."

But this ad hoc development and piecemeal legislative patching, excusable when income tax formed an inconsiderable part of the revenue, was fiscally dangerous now the tax had become the major contributor: there was a need for reviewing the whole of the income tax law. To this end, after the Consolidation Act of 1918, an essential preliminary, a Royal Commission on Income Tax was set up "to enquire into the Income Tax (including Supertax) of the United Kingdom in all its aspects including the scope, rates and incidence of the tax: allowances and reliefs: administration, assessment, appeal and collection: and prevention of evasion: and to rport what alterations of law and practice are necessary."

Its recommendations on differentiation, graduation and allowances were soon translated into law. The fraction of one-tenth was adopted for earned income relief with a maximum of £200: the suggested reduced rate relief up to £225 of taxable income at one-half standard rate was introduced: and the proposed allowances came in at intervals during the twenties. Such reforms are instantly recognisable. Far more fascinating is to trace the subsequent history of some recommendations not immediately adopted, for example the abolition of the office of assessor, the appointment of Collectors by the Board of Inland Revenue and the waning of the General Commissioners' powers to those of a purely appellate body. The changes in capital allowances under the Income Tax Act 1945 originated with the Commission's deliberations on the depreciation of plant and buildings: benefits in kind came under review: but a praiseworthy attempt to define trading still awaits legislation as an ever-lengthening line of tax cases testifies. Its robust commonsense, its exhaustive research and patient investigation, enshrined in two foolscap volumes of evidence and a third embodying the Report itself, have rarely been equalled and never excelled by any similar Commission.

Apart from the 1920 Budget which implemented the recommendations of the Royal Commission thus marking the end of war finance as well as shaping modern income tax for a generation or more, the other Budgets of the Twenties matched neither the inspiration of the 1920 proposals nor the pace and violence of political events. The first three chased a fading vision of economy, although Baldwin in 1925 did manage a decrease in standard rate, which automatically aroused the anger of the Labour Party as the remissions, in Ramsay MacDonald's words, "would be spent on unnecessary and parasitical forms of luxury."

The fourth budget of the period was the first produced by the Labour Party. In the circumstances of a minority government it could hardly be a truly Socialist measure: indeed its sole concession to Labour (and Liberal) ideals was a reduction in indirect taxation, for there was no nationalisation, no capital levy and no "soaking of the rich". Snowden in office was very different from Snowden in opposition. He is reported to have asked "with a Treasury Clerk's intonation 'Where was the money to come from?'" during a discussion on public works which he firmly believed should pay for themselves.

The final five budgets were the work of Churchill. They contained some useful amendments to income tax law such as the adoption of the previous year basis of assessment for both Schedules D and E, and some reductions in direct taxation which provoked the reaction from Snowden that it (the 1925 Bill) "was the worst rich man's Budget that was ever proposed"; but in spite of the Chancellor's rhetorical skill and fiscal ingenuity, both of which were considerable, he could not finally conceal the fact that he was fighting a losing battle against an economic situation which the Tory Government had largely devised by returning to the gold standard in 1925. Income tax had helped to fight a war: no Chancellor, however, looked back to Peel's example of how to use it to win a peace. For by 1929 Snowden, Chancellor again, was in the grip of economic furies he could neither control nor understand and to which he could only oppose his cautious, orthodox emphasis on direct taxation, without any attempt to encourage an industrial revival by making it more selective. He could not indeed foresee the completeness and duration of the coming collapse: but even by the time of his fourth budget in 1931, when he was pledged to economy by the Committee chaired by Sir George May, an ex-Secretary of the Prudential Insurance Company, of his increased levies 70 per cent was direct and 30 per cent indirect.

The years from 1933 to 1945 saw more radical changes in direct taxation and in budgetary policy than any period of the same length in British fiscal history. Neville Chamberlain's first four budgets show a gradual emergence from the shadow of Snowden's austerity, although he flatly refused at any stage to unbalance the budget deliberately: but aided by a limited economic revival he was able to give slight relief to both industry in 1934 and the individual in 1935. His last three budgets were inevitably constrained by rising expenditure on armaments, a handicap which intensified under John Simon, Chancellor in Chamberlain's Government of 1937–40. But even when war broke out the level of taxation at first hardly took on an emergency aspect. It was left to Kingsley Wood and his advisers, especially Keynes, to put taxation on a war footing so that income tax, with the improved mechanism of Pay As You Earn introduced in 1943 increased its yield from £371 millions in 1938 to £1,426 millions in 1945; while the new excess profits tax at 100 per cent brought in close on £500 millions at its maximum. The effect of its penal rates was cushioned for both profits and wages by a system of post-war credits, the brain-child of Keynes. Finally Anderson, the fourth Chancellor of the period, completed the transformation of the budget from a book-keeping statement of income and expenditure to its use as a cardinal instrument of government policy; and, equally important, he switched from direct taxation, commonly assumed to have reached its limit, to a greater emphasis on indirect and introduced the revised system of capital allowances which modified high rates of taxation by granting increased relief for modernisation and re-equipment.

Labour's fiscal policy on taking office in 1945 was summarised on its manifesto "Let Us Face The Future" as "taxation bearing less on low income groups". Industry and the individual both benefited, the former by a decrease in standard rate, in the excess profits tax rate, and the introduction of the new code of capital allowances, and the latter also by standard rate decrease, balanced however by an increase in surtax rates, and the stepping up of allowances. Hugh Dalton persisted with this policy of relaxation of income tax as did Cripps, his successor, offsetting this now somewhat muted relief by a mild experiment in capital levy known as the special contribution levied on investment income over £250 and graduated from 2s. to 10s. in the pound: it was a 'one-off' for 1947–8. Gaitskill concluded this period of Labour rule with his first and last budget in 1951: faced with a massive new defence progreamme, caused by the Korean crisis, and a worsening economic situation, an increase in income tax rates could not be avoided. It was in some ways the end of an era which had over-emphasised direct taxation.

It was now the turn of the Tories. Excess war profits were to be creamed off by excess profits levy, a watered-down version of the wartime excess profits tax, for the period of the emergency: but the plan for income tax was centred round R.A. Butler's belief that "the present weight of direct taxation is a very positive discouragement to extra effort." Direct taxation could hardly be a primary mechanism for the control of the crises which had affected the British economy in 1947, 1949 and 1951: the Chancellor's expansionist policy, however, coincided with, if it did not altogether cause, a limited period of recovery.

Meanwhile, after a twenty-year gap, the theory of taxation was again under review in the Tucker and Radcliffe Reports. The former which reported in 1931 was concerned solely with the taxation of trading profits: and the virtue of expediency inspired their mainly administrative recommendations, many of which were incorporated in the legislation of the succeeding three years: but as the Committee confessed there were "no startling contributions to the universally desired simplification." The latter, however, was a far more ambitious project with much wider terms of reference, "the present system of taxation of profits and income, including its incidence and effects." The Reports were published in April 1954 and June 1955, the first dealing with the PAYE system and the familiar themes of graduation and differentiation and the second (final) Report with every other aspect of the direct taxation system. Despite the vast amount of evidence and the ninety recommendations, there was no proposal to make any basic change in the current income tax code. Only the minority Report, two of the signatories of which were Kaldor and Woodcock, broke the calm conservatism: for they put forward the apparent heresies of a capital gains tax and a corporation profits tax.

Very much after the Dalton pattern, Butler followed his 1952 relief to the individual the following year with allowances to industry, the reduction of standard rate and the proposed repeal of excess profits levy in 1954. From that date, the high-water mark of "Butskillism", there was an increasing polarisation between Conservative and Labour, the latter taking the view that companies were proving to be the "favourite children" and "the larger the income, the greater the benefits." There was no more agreement amongst economists on the correct course to pursue. At least, during the Butler period, there was a coherent mainly controlled inflationary policy: when MacMillan succeeded him in 1955 it became increasingly difficult to trace any fiscal pattern, possibly because there were five very different Chancellors in office from 1956 to 1964 each of whom pursued a course of spasmodic remission and retrenchment, stop-go as it was currently termed in both allowances and rates: the only real innovations were Lloyd's introduction of a short-term gains tax in 1962 and Maudling's proposal in his 1963 Budget of "free depreciation", the writing-off of capital expenditure provided for industrial purposes in areas of high unemployment in one year.

There was, however, one aspect of taxation which needed ever-increasing attention. Taxation and evasion are complementary twins and resistance to fiscal levies had a long and not always dishonourable history from Wat Tyler to Hampden. But when parliamentary control over revenue had been won the word evasion acquired a more sinister ring. Pitt had complained in 1799 that income tax was forced on him by the frauds which had devalued the assessed taxes, but the technique then, and again when income tax was re-imposed in 1842, consisted of the comparatively unsophisticated method of either omitting assessable items or scaling down their amount. Both the Hume (1851) and the Hubbard (1861) Committees discussed the evasion problem but the "stringent powers" needed to create it ran counter to current political thinking. In any case, as a matter of practical economics, if not of public morality, the lowness of rates meant the actual loss of income was inconsiderable. The Boer War, however, forced the problem of evasion into the open and inspired the Ritchie (an Ex-Chancellor) Committee of 1905, the only Committee on taxation to deal exclusively with "the prevention of fraud and evasion". It found, in brief, that there was "abundant evidence to show ... there is a substantial amount of fraud and evasion ... serious enough to demand some amendment of law and practice."

It was in the evidence of the Select Committee of 1906 that the ominous phrase "legal avoidance" first appeared and for the past seventy years the most complex Regulation in any Finance Act has been reserved for the countering of avoidance. Not that the process had gone very far by World War I: and, although the excess profits duty of that period had built-in safety precautions against avoidance, the 1920 Committee concerned itself, in that context, with mere evasion. Regulation against artificial transactions was suggested: but the form of blanket proposal envisaged cannot be so simply administered in practice. Admittedly there were specific sections against specific devices: when, however, it was always conceded that "the subject is entitled so to arrange his affairs so as not to attract taxes as far as he can legitimately do", it was not surprising that the government confessed "the way of the man who tries to stop up the holes of the tax evader without hitting the innocent is extraordinarily difficult". Even so, pre-World War II avoidance was an art rather than an industry: and that, broadly speaking, remained true during World War II, with the effective anti-avoidance provisions of excess profits tax and the days of austerity up to the Fifties.

Then the pace and ingenuity of avoidance devices quickened from artificial cessations to elaborations of bond-washing and dividend-stripping until it was necessary in 1960 to propose the most technical Finance Bill in the whole history of income tax which, with its three general avoidance sections, aroused some fears of an over-mighty bureaucracy. For the danger now was not mere avoidance of tax but the securing of repayments of duty which had never in fact been paid. Fortunately there was an acceptable course between often tardy corrective regulation and discretionary bureaucratic powers. A number of avoidance devices consisted basically of the manipulation of years of assessment or the conversion of apparently revenue into capital profits: both these escape routes could be blocked by a corporation profits tax, where assessment and accounting year would coincide, and a capital gains tax respectively: and both these solutions, under active consideration at least since the minority report of the Radcliffe Committee, were embodied in a Finance Act in 1965 of 271 pages, 97 clauses and 22 Schedules, including the new Schedule F which made the deduction of tax from dividends a reality.

But even with this massive addition to statute, the flood of fiscal Regulation showed no sign of abating. Admittedly there was a certain lull up to 1970 when material from the Income Tax Act 1952 and some twenty later Acts was consolidated into the Income and Corporation Tax Act 1970 and the Taxes Management Act 1970: this completed the work begun with the Capital Allowances Act 1968. The succeeding year saw the unification of income tax and surtax and a revised method of granting capital allowances, followed in 1972 by the replacement of the "classical" system of corporation tax, which preserved a complete separation between a company and its shareholders with an imputation system which releases tax on the distributed profits as a credit against shareholder's own liability: these were the Conservative Government's last fiscal measures.

The final years before the Labour Government resigned saw the inception of three new taxes. These were, firstly the petroleum revenue tax, a potential money-spinner, which is currently being increased to 70 per cent with advanced payment provisions. The second was capital transfer tax, replacing the old estate duty which had survived, virtually unchanged, since Harcourts' revision of 1894. Basically it remained the old estate duty with gift tax sections welded on the front end, but with no accession element. Finally there was development land tax, the latest in a long line of attempts to find an efficient means of taxing land: starting with Lloyd George in 1909, the statute book is littered with planning Acts, betterment levies and development gains taxation, none of which ever achieved their ostensible aims.

There were also major changes in Schedule E and the introduction of stock relief to cushion the effect of inflation. Finally, in Mr. Healey's last year of office, he managed to make numerous changes in every aspect of taxation including retrospective legislation against commodity-dealing and relief for profit-sharing schemes. The government also suffered two notable defeats over the amount of basic rate and the higher rate threshold: but, to end on a note of chivalry, a start was made on removing discrimination against women who had for far too long been included under the unromantic heading of "incapacitated persons" along with infants and persons of unsound mind.

There was certainly no lack of legislation: what was missing was a coherent fiscal policy over the period; and the Budgets, for all their technicality, were basically ad hoc, being tailored to fit the particular circumstances of the time. For instance there was no attempt to check Government spending until the intervention of the IMF: and it is hard to imagine what Mr. Healey's predecessors would have made of his promise to reduce taxation in return for a unions' undertaking to abate their wage claims.

It was inevitable that the fiscal policy of the new Government should show some radical shifts: and the present Chancellor, Sir Geoffrey Howe's, first Budget could be described as a classical Conservative Budget in the swing from direct to indirect taxation exemplified by the raising of the rate of VAT to 15 per cent., just 10 per cent below the lowest rate of direct taxation. From this base, and over the life of the present Parliament, the Chancellor has three main objectives – to cut down the public sector borrowing requirements, to leave more money free, an old Gladstonian maxim, and to encourage the small business, a process tentatively commenced by Labour. There is no indication yet of any attempt to incorporate the thinking of the Meade Report of 1978, except perhaps the swingeing VAT increase, to check the "black economy", or to curb the increasing obscurity of legislation: currently in the pipeline are changes in the capital taxes and in the assessment of benefits, a challenging but worrying prospect. Whatever the vicissitudes of the economic scene, taxation still remains a growth industry.

The now accepted duty of the government to regulate the economy implies the use of political considerations, both nationally and internationally, as a fiscal yardstick. In general, as current trends illustrate, the Conservatives have tended to favour indirect taxation and the providing of incentives by relieving industry and the higher rate taxpayer. Labour inclines to direct taxation and finding ways, a difficult process, out of the poverty trap. Both parties have regarded avoidance as socially unacceptable: they have legislated against it impartially in turn without really succeeding in coping with the difficulty of translating the economic concept of taxable income into legislative sense. Both parties have been equally guilty of manipulating the levers of a fiscal system whose very efficiency is a temptation

146

to the extremists of both sides. Yet it remains a remarkable feature of current fiscal trends that, despite the ever-increasing amount of fiscal literature, the annual Finance Act is still, in the main, the work of pragmatists.

The past nine hundred years of tax legislation, becoming gradually more complex over the last century and a half as social and economic life became equally complex have resulted in probably the most elaborate tax structure in fiscal history. The system is administered by an army of government servants and monitored on behalf of the taxpayer by a parallel number of legal and accountancy experts. Yet behind these formidable intricacies, refined and reinforced annually by at least one Finance Act, lies, in the case of direct taxation, where it matters most, a straightforward right of appeal to alternative bodies of Commissioners one of which is purely amateur. Whether the point at issue relates to a scenario of avoidance or the simple non-allowance of some relief, the whole apparatus of Revenue officials, accountants and solicitors fades into the background and the case can be determined by an informal procedure which has hardly changed since 1799: and the jurisdiction is still that of local Commissioners who can trace their lineage back, through the eighteenth century Land Tax Commissioners, to those early juries of neighbours in the days when income tax was poll tax, when the only land tax was scutage and duties on estates simply the feudal obligations due to the lord in his castle high above the mediaeval village.